Grade A

Résumés
for Teachers

Third Edition

101

Grade A

Résumés
for Teachers
Third Edition

by Rebecca Anthony and Gerald Roe

BARRON'S

ABOUT THE AUTHORS

Rebecca Jespersen Anthony and Gerald Roe are career specialists at The University of Iowa. They have written numerous articles on employment and the job search, with an emphasis on academic careers. Authors of seven books, including *The Curriculum Vitae Handbook* and *Over 40 and Looking for Work,* they have developed specialized training packets for career professionals and have co-directed national studies dealing with employment and hiring issues in education.

The authors have served in leadership positions in professional associations and are frequent presenters at conferences and seminars.

DEDICATED TO

Tas, Natalya, Jess, Tassie, Veronica,

Steve, April, Dave,

Anthony, Allison

Always, with kind thoughts
of Penelope, in Wyoming.

All inquiries should be addressed to:
Barron's Educational Series, Inc.
250 Wireless Boulevard
Hauppauge, New York 11788
www.barronseduc.com

ISBN-13: 978-0-7641-1987-7
ISBN-10: 0-7641-1987-3

Library of Congress Catalog Card No.: 2003044416

Library of Congress Cataloging-in-Publication Data
Anthony, Rebecca, 1950-
    101 Grade A résumés for teachers / Rebecca Anthony and Gerald Roe.—3rd ed.
      p.   cm.
    On title page the 0 in 101 is represented by an "apple."
    ISBN 0-7641-1987-7
    1. Teachers—Employment. 2. Résumés (Employment) 3. Cover letters.
  I. Title: One hundred one grade A résumés for teachers. II. Title: One hundred and one grade A résumés for teachers. III. Roe, Gerald. IV. Title

  LB1780.A677 2003
  808'.06665—dc21
                         2003044416

PRINTED IN THE UNITED STATES OF AMERICA
987654

CONTENTS

PREFACE

When we first decided to write a book about résumés for teachers, it was not because there was any shortage of books about résumés. Any good bookstore can provide numerous books about résumé preparation, with countless sample résumés in various formats. Recent additions to the literature include advice about designing digitized résumés to be posted on the Internet or using key words to attract the attention of an impartial and inanimate electronic scanner. But when teachers look into these books, they seldom find themselves reflected there, although in sheer numbers—not to mention the significance of what they do—teachers comprise a substantial portion of the workforce. According to the National Center for Education Statistics, there are more than 3.2 million classroom teachers today, with a projected 3.35 million within the decade. Teachers deserve a book about résumé preparation that is designed expressly for them.

An educator's résumé is only superficially like résumés in the business sector. Not only is the vocabulary of a teacher's résumé different from that of other occupations, even within the profession there is considerable variation from state to state and from region to region. Similarly, a teacher's achievement is not measured in quite the same way. Teachers and school administrators cannot rely on numbers to document efficiency or to prove productivity. Promotion is not a real issue for the classroom teacher, and profitability cannot and must not be the bottom line.

The idea for this book grew out of more than twenty years of work with thousands of new and experienced teachers. Response to the first and second editions indicates that beginners and veteran educators have found the book of genuine help in promoting their various skills and qualifications to potential employers. We believe that educators at every level can find themselves reflected in these pages and can use the samples to let employers know about their skills and qualifications.

PART ONE

YOUR RÉSUMÉ

1
WHAT IS A RÉSUMÉ?

A résumé is a summary of experience. That's all it is, just a summary of experience. It is not a technical blueprint, an autobiography, a testament, or an essay. A résumé is not a legal document, nor is it a formal declaration prepared according to standard specifications. Computer generated or typewritten, printed or electronically stored and retrieved, a résumé is a summary of experience—period.

Myths and mysteries have grown up around the subject, making many people, particularly those who are preparing to write their first résumé, think they face a task of great difficulty. Consequently, they procrastinate, they copy the first model they see, or they try to find someone to prepare a résumé for them.

WHO KNOWS YOU BEST?

The truth is, *you* are the expert. You are the person best qualified to put yourself on paper. Considering the importance of a résumé in today's marketplace, you would be foolish to allow anyone else to do it for you. No one can do it better.

Even if you are just beginning your career in education, you have found many occasions to create a paper profile. You filled out applications to be admitted to college and more forms to enter a teacher preparation program. You know how to provide information to the Internal Revenue Service, a bank, a financial aid office, a credit card company. You could almost consider yourself an expert at filling out forms.

Unfortunately, you may never escape the struggle to fit the shape of your life into a form of someone else's devising. But preparing a résumé is less complicated and far more interesting than merely filling out forms. In the first place, *you* get to decide what's most important. You decide what you want to highlight; you even decide what you'd just as soon not call to anyone's attention. You control the presentation, you design the format, and you create your best professional image.

FITTING INTO PRESCRIPTIVE MODELS

All of the information you will use to build your résumé could be forced to fit neatly or awkwardly into various prescribed models. Traditionally, two principal types of résumé have been touted and promoted: chronological and functional. Lengthy discussions of their differences, and their inherent advantages and disadvantages, have been carried on among career development professionals in books and articles and more recently in electronic bulletin boards and news groups.

Briefly, a chronological résumé takes a historical approach. The résumé focuses on dates and locations, listing educational background and work record, including job titles and names of employers. A functional résumé, on the other hand, emphasizes competencies, abilities, and achievements without necessarily relating them to a specific work experience or time frame.

Too often, strict adherence to either model will limit an educator's ability to make the most advantageous presentation. Each model has features that can capture the reader's attention and promote specific strengths. The most effective features of chronological and functional approaches can be combined in a résumé that emphasizes your unique personal and professional attributes.

Personal computers have made résumé preparation much easier than ever before. With a personal computer and a letter-quality printer, you can create an attractive and effective résumé. Updates are simple, and you can develop different versions to emphasize particular strengths or experiences as they relate to the specific position you are interested in.

Many software programs offer résumé assistance. Be cautious about adopting a template or following too closely a résumé model that does not meet your needs. Some packaged programs are flexible enough to allow you to select fonts of varying sizes and types; others have preset fonts for your name, contact information, and category headings. A few minutes with any résumé software package will usually allow you to determine if it offers sufficient flexibility to serve your purpose, to present your special skills and abilities, and to project your best image.

No single prescribed model should dictate the format, arrangement, or organization of your résumé. Common sense, combined with your particular priorities, should be the hallmark of your presentation.

2
EDUCATORS NEED RÉSUMÉS

Like professionals in many other fields—marketing, finance, engineering, medicine, science, government, and social service—educators need to know how to prepare and use a résumé. But different professions require different approaches, different treatments, different vocabularies. A résumé must be particularly suited to the profession as well as to the individual. A model résumé for a marketing director will be of no help to a third grade teacher.

A marketing résumé must reflect a business image. Accomplishments and potential should be described in terms of increased sales, reduced expenses, improved productivity, time saved, and advancement from one position to another. Stating accomplishments in terms of dollars and cents, percentages, increases and decreases, and profits and losses is reasonable and effective.

A teacher's résumé, however, only superficially resembles the typical business model. The focus, the emphasis, the vocabulary, and the overall message are different. Teachers should not attempt to follow the dictates of other occupations. The result will not strike the appropriate tone, nor will it focus on educational objectives. Teachers do not have a product, educational progress is not always and not necessarily measured in percentages, promotion is hardly an issue, and profitability is not the bottom line.

KNOW YOUR CULTURE

Caution: Each profession has its own culture, its own way of doing things, and to some extent its own language—certainly its own jargon. Do not use the language or techniques of another occupation to seek a teaching position. It is all too easy to adopt catchy terms and fashionable phrases, but educators must take care to stay within their own culture. Inappropriate use of popular buzz words can signal a lack of understanding of the profession or a misguided attempt to appear more knowledgeable or more qualified.

Even within the field of education, terminology is not uniform. Because each state has the responsibility of providing a system of public instruction for its citizens, the vocabulary and the definition of conditions, programs, and services is not uniform throughout the country.

The terminology used in a particular state to describe a teaching specialization may be quite different from terms used even in neighboring states. Each state approves educational programs for its schools, determines requirements for certification, and issues licenses for teachers and administrators.

The problem is compounded by abbreviations and acronyms referring to teacher preparation programs, modes of instruction, and organizational systems. Although you may be familiar with several of these common abbreviations, you cannot assume that your reader will understand what is meant by IEP, CLP, BD, ELD, ED, LD, ESL, TOEFL, MR, MMMI, MH, BH, ADD, ADHD, AEA, CESA. Instead of using abbreviations, it is a good idea to spell out the terms, especially if you send your résumé to employers in other states.

SELF-PROMOTION IS GOOD PRACTICE

All successful job seekers have marketing plans. Teachers, too, must learn how to promote themselves, how to sell their skills and abilities to employers. Your challenge is to create a professionally appropriate résumé; a résumé that reflects your culture and that promotes you as a committed educator with experiences and abilities that are—if not unique—clearly consistent with current practices and procedures.

The first résumé you write will most likely be used in a job search. As your career develops, you will find many other occasions to prepare and submit a résumé. A résumé is an essential document for every educator at every stage of a career.

A good résumé is an indispensable marketing tool for:

- student teachers
- first-year teachers
- experienced teachers

And for:

- substitute teachers
- paraprofessionals

And for:

- supervisors
- consultants
- principals
- superintendents

Whether you are a novice or a veteran, if you are or if you want to become one of these educators, you need a résumé.

3
WHAT GOES INTO A RÉSUMÉ?

A résumé is built on facts: facts about you, your education, your background, your experiences. A good résumé presents the facts in a logical and meaningful sequence, telling potential employers who you are and what you have done, capturing their interest, and leading them to the desired conclusion that you are a candidate for a personal interview.

Forcing the reader to solve a puzzle or unravel a mystery story deprives you of the opportunity to make a good first impression. You rarely have the luxury of a second chance.

THREE ESSENTIALS

Start with the basics. Be sure to include clear and direct information about these three essential items:

1. Identity
    Use your legal name, your full address, and your telephone number. Zip codes and area codes are important. So are FAX numbers and E-mail addresses. This information seems obvious, but personnel departments and hiring officials frequently receive résumés lacking an address or other contact information.

2. Educational Background
    List academic degrees earned or in progress, major or field of study in which degrees were earned, and dates conferred or expected. Accuracy and honesty are critical.

3. Teaching Experience
    Any teaching experience (including full- or part-time professional experience, student teaching, practica, and internships) can be included on a résumé. Substantial professional experience can make it unnecessary to list early training experiences.

COMPILING RÉSUMÉ FACTS

Take a few minutes to fill in the blanks with facts about yourself. Once you have listed these basics, you will have all the material you need to begin working on a draft of your résumé.

Identification

Name _____

Records under other names _____

Address _____

Telephone _____

FAX Number _____

E-mail Address _____

URL Internet Address _____

It may be necessary to list both a temporary and a permanent address. It is permissible to indicate a termination date for the temporary address: for example, until June 1.

Education

Degree-granting institutions: _____

Institution and Location _____

Attended from: _____ to: _____

Degree earned or in progress _____

Graduation date _____

Major: _____ Minor: _____

Area(s) of specialization: _____

_____

Institution and Location _____

Attended from: _____ to: _____

Degree earned or in progress _____

Graduation date _____

Major: _____ Minor: _____

Area(s) of specialization: _____

_____

Other institutions attended: _____

Institution and Location _____

Attended from: _____ to: _____

Major: _____ Minor: _____

Area(s) of specialization: _____

_____

Institution and Location _____

Attended from: _____ to: _____

Major: _____ Minor: _____

Area(s) of specialization: _____

_____

Teaching Experience

Information about internship experience or student teaching is essential for beginners and optional for teachers with professional experience. After more than a year or two of professional experience, information about preprofessional experience is generally included only if it indicates a different area of expertise or a significantly different grade level.

Position: _____

Employer: _____

Name and location of school or organization

Dates of Employment: _____ to: _____

Accomplishments: _____

_____

_____

Position: _____

Employer: _____

Name and location of school or organization

Dates of Employment: _____ to: _____

Accomplishments: _____

_____

_____

BUT I HAVEN'T DONE ANYTHING SPECIAL...

Once you have completed the three basic sections, you might wonder what other information you need to incorporate. Procrastination can easily set in if you are convinced that you don't have anything but the basics to put into a résumé. Don't take this shortsighted view. You have a multitude of possibilities for additional sections. All teachers, beginners and experienced alike, have many special achievements, accomplishments, and significant experiences to relate.

Yes, everyone else completed student teaching or an internship. But no one had your particular experience. No one else achieved the same things, taught the same units, developed your unique style of teaching, or motivated the students in quite the same way. Very few people have taken exactly the same course work as you or had identical job or volunteer experiences.

It is a mistake to assume that your experiences are ordinary. Any hiring official will assume you have spent some time in a classroom in order to earn a teaching license. But no assumptions can be made about your achievements, your successes, your singular approach to good teaching. It is up to you to let your strengths be known.

A Special Note: Be careful not to overlook any unusual educational experiences. Special programs, summer institutes, foreign study tours, or a semester or year abroad can capture an employer's attention and make your résumé stand out from the others in the pile. Most employers realize that educators who seek these supplemental experiences tend to be independent, intellectually curious, and committed to learning.

WHAT, NOT WHEN

Don't be unduly influenced by dates. What you have done is certainly more important than when you did it. For example, honors or other special recognitions rarely lose their impact. If you were inducted into Phi Beta Kappa twenty years ago, you can still consider this distinction a relevant item for your résumé. Being selected student body president or outstanding history student or receiving the Volunteer of the Year award retains value long after the recognition was bestowed.

MORE FACTS...

If you are looking for additional facts for your résumé, the following checklist can help you recall previous experiences and activities. Quickly read through the list and check as many *Yes* responses as you can. Then come back and jot down the specifics. Don't worry about when it happened or the level of importance at this point. Don't worry about vocabulary and phrasing, either; just record the basic information. When you're ready to write a rough draft of your résumé, you can develop full-fledged entries based on your responses. Prioritizing, refining the language, and polishing the individual sections will come later.

Yes No

❏ ❏ Language abilities

_____

_____

❏ ❏ Technology skills

_____

_____

❏ ❏ Professional web site

_____

_____

❏ ❏ Study or travel abroad

_____

_____

Yes No

❑ ❑ Professional memberships/elected offices

_____

_____

❑ ❑ Leadership positions (campus/community)

_____

_____

❑ ❑ Conference attendance/participation

_____

_____

❑ ❑ Volunteer activities/civic contributions

_____

_____

❑ ❑ Professional recognition

_____

_____

❑ ❑ Honors, awards, distinctions

_____

_____

❑ ❑ College activities

_____

_____

❑ ❑ Avocations and interests

_____

_____

❑ ❑ Community service/service learning

_____

_____

❑ ❑ Exhibits, shows, publications

_____

_____

Yes No

❑ ❑ Grants, special projects

_____

_____

❑ ❑ Teaching competencies

_____

_____

❑ ❑ Extracurricular interests

_____

_____

❑ ❑ Professional development

_____

_____

❑ ❑ Recent courses of interest

_____

_____

❑ ❑ GPA (overall and major)

_____

_____

❑ ❑ Other work

_____

_____

❑ ❑ Other

_____

_____

DO I NEED A JOB OBJECTIVE?

In some occupations, a job objective is both traditional and useful; consequently, many people consider a job objective indispensable and expect to see it right at the top of the résumé. As an educator, however, you can convey a professional objective in a number of ways. You can express your interests, preferences, or priorities as *Teaching Competencies*, *Teaching Interests*, or *Special Skills*. Training in multiple teaching techniques, strategies, or methods and exposure to different teaching styles or settings can be communicated to a potential employer at a glance. Other sections of your résumé reinforce your objective and help convince the reader of your competence or expertise.

A useful job objective is clear, specific, and unencumbered with extraneous words. If you include an explicit statement of your job objective, restrict it to the nature of the position:

Head basketball coach

Journalism teacher and student newspaper advisor

Bilingual kindergarten teacher

A note of caution: Too often, objectives look like this:

Objective: To obtain a position that is challenging, rewarding, and affords opportunity for personal growth and professional development.

Examine that statement. What does it say? And what message does it send? A close look reveals a mere series of words and phrases that are correct and proper and good and safe but have no real significance. They sound prefabricated if not pretentious. This calculated objective is too general to be of any use and is simply a waste of your space and the reader's time.

EVALUATING AND SELECTING

Look at all the things you have listed and select those entries that contribute to the image or picture you want to present to potential employers. Not everything is of equal value or importance, and you may decide that some items are no longer relevant and do not justify using space that could be taken by more current or more pertinent information.

Carefully and thoughtfully select items that emphasize your strongest assets and greatest interests.

ARRANGING YOUR INFORMATION

As you look over your list of facts and previous experiences, you will see that some of them can naturally be grouped together. Your résumé can have several sections representing different aspects of your educational background, interests, and experience. Each section can be assigned a descriptive heading to attract and to direct the reader's attention.

As you organize your material, the following list can help you select appropriate headings for the sections or divisions of your résumé.

SUGGESTED HEADINGS FOR YOUR RÉSUMÉ

Degree(s)

Educational Background

Education

Educational Preparation

Academic Training

Study Abroad

Course Highlights

Courses of Interest

Academic Highlights

Course Concentration

Teaching Certificate(s)
Certificate(s)
License(s)
Licensure
Endorsements
Coaching Certification
Other Certification

Career Objective
Teaching Objective
Job Objective
Objective
Professional Objective
Position Desired

Teaching Strengths
Skills and Competencies
Teaching Competencies
Teaching Skills
Teaching Interests
Areas of Expertise
Areas of Knowledge
Special Skills
Special Talent

Computer Training
Multimedia Expertise
Technology Skills

Teaching Experience
Professional Experience
Classroom Experience
Teaching Overview
Experience Highlights
Related Experiences
Student Teaching
Internship Experience
Practicum Experience
Practica
Field Experiences

Professional Seminars
Workshops Attended
Special Training
In-service Training
Professional Activities
Current Activities
Exhibits
Shows
Performances
Publications
Presentations
Conference Participation
Seminar Presentations

Language Competencies
Language Ability
Languages
Travel Abroad
Travel
Overseas Travel
Foreign Experiences
International Experiences
Overseas Study

Professional Leadership
Professional Memberships
Affiliations
Professional Societies
Honorary Societies
College Distinctions
College Activities
Special Recognition
Academic Honors
Achievements
Honors and Distinctions
Awards
Scholarships

Extracurricular Interests
Coaching Skills

Coaching Interests	Employment
Club Advisor	Other Work
Class Sponsor	Part-time Work
	Summer Work Experience
Service	Additional Experience
Committee Responsibilities	Nonteaching Experience
Committee Assignments	Military Service
Departmental Service	Other Experiences
Civic Contributions	
Community Service	Portfolio
Community Activities	Electronic Portfolio
Civic Activities	On-line Portfolio
Community Involvement	
Volunteer Activities	References
Activities	Credentials
Leisure Activities	Credential File
Avocations	Placement File
Interests	

BREAKING THE ONE-PAGE RULE

Teachers often need more than one page to present a complete account of their qualifications, especially if they have professional experience in the classroom. Depending on the number of field-based experiences, even a beginner may find it necessary to use more than a single page.

By contrast, people in the business world usually try to restrict a résumé to a single page. A new graduate in finance or accounting would consider a second page unconventional and likely to create an unfavorable impression. Even a person with considerable experience might hesitate to expand to a second page. So powerful is the mystique surrounding a single-page résumé that even people who should not be bound by this rule are afraid to abandon it.

Quantity alone, however, is not the goal. There is such a thing as padding: overzealous descriptions, annotations that pile detail upon insignificant detail, or long tedious lists of the most minute or routine activities can have the effect of trivializing every aspect of the résumé. Fit all relevant information on a single page if you can, but do not be afraid of offending the reader by expanding your resume beyond this arbitrary limit.

The goal of a résumé is to stimulate interest, not to overwhelm with detail. A résumé should be as long as it needs to be and as short as it can be.

Employers in education are more inclined to focus on the content than on the length. And they will be more favorably impressed with a résumé that is easy to read and pleasing to the eye.

4
WHAT
GETS
LEFT OUT?

Contrary to what you may have heard, it is unnecessary to list every activity, include details of every experience, or account for every year. Your résumé is not your permanent record, your autobiography, or a blueprint for your future.

Ambitions, dreams, speculations, long-range plans, and ultimate goals have their place in a job search. But they don't belong on your résumé.

BE CONSISTENT

Your résumé must agree with all information provided to an employer, but it does not have to duplicate other documents or contain every bit of data on your educational background. Employers will ask for your transcript, which will list all courses taken as well as grades earned and degrees conferred. Grade point average is not a standard entry on a teacher's résumé.

In the initial screening process, most hiring officials are not overly concerned with your grade point average. They scan your résumé to find evidence of your educational qualifications, your teaching experiences, and your demonstrated interest in working with children or youth. Unlike some employers in the business sector, school officials do not restrict serious consideration to candidates with a predetermined grade point average. Good grades are always an asset, never a detriment. But scholastic achievement is valued in combination with other special skills you can offer in the classroom. A high GPA does not guarantee that you will work successfully with children.

If your educational record gives the impression that you were a peripatetic student roving from campus to campus, you might want to list on your résumé only the institution that granted your degree. This is not a technique to deceive employers but a way to save valuable space to promote your teaching abilities. You are not obligated to list on your résumé every institution you have attended. The school district's application form will likely request a complete educational record, and your official transcripts will show attendance at all institutions from which you have transferred credits.

WHAT ABOUT REFERENCES?

The initial screening process usually does not require names and addresses of individual references, and you need not waste space or time in providing them. Application forms almost always ask for references; there is no advantage to duplicating this information or providing names and addresses before they are requested.

If a job announcement specifically asks for names and addresses of references, you may choose to list them at the end of your résumé, make a separate reference listing page, or include their names and contact information in your application letter. Always get permission to list a person as a reference.

Give a copy of your current résumé to each person who has agreed to serve as a reference for you. The résumé will help your recommender to provide accurate information regarding your experiences and abilities.

CUTTING OUT THE DEADWOOD

Experienced professionals should carefully review information about preprofessional training. Retaining outdated information can increase the length but not the impact of your résumé. Lists of practica or student teaching experiences that occurred several years ago are seldom worth the space they occupy. Moreover, they can divert attention from recent and more important professional development.

Activities dating back to high school or even college years may have little relevance to your current objective and are probably best omitted. There are always exceptions to this rule, however. For example, if you are qualified and interested in promoting yourself as a basketball coach but did not play on a college team, you could reach back to high school and briefly mention your participation in team sports. If you were an all-conference player or selected to an all-state team, the information will add some credibility to your potential as a coach. Similar examples could be given for yearbook sponsorship, cheerleading, debate, or any other school activity. If you are seeking a teaching position at a preparatory school or a parochial institution, it is probably a good idea to mention that you attended a similar school.

Your résumé is not an official document; you have the opportunity and the responsibility to determine the facts you want to present and the skills you want to emphasize.

DON'T WRITE YOUR AUTOBIOGRAPHY

During the selection process, all information requested by an employer should be job related. Hiring officials should not solicit information about marital or family status, disabilities, age, gender, race, ethnic background, religion, height, weight, or color of eyes and hair. Obviously, this personal data is not job related. Because it does not affect your qualifications or your potential as an educator, there is no reason for you to volunteer this kind of information.

Providing unsolicited personal data to employers may be a detriment to yourself and to the employer. Federal and state guidelines prohibit employers from requesting preemployment information of this sort. Applicants who supply this type of information actually place a burden on the employers who must devise procedures to discount potentially discriminatory information.

DON'T CLUTTER YOUR RÉSUMÉ WITH NONESSENTIALS

Space on your résumé is valuable. Include only those items that can help you to promote your skills and abilities to potential employers. Don't squander space on irrelevant information. The employer will see it as a waste of time and interpret it as your inability to organize thoughts and data.

Your résumé does not need and should not contain these items:

1. *Title.* Reserve the most prominent location for your name. The reader will recognize a résumé without seeing the word "RÉSUMÉ" as the first line of the first page. Keep the focus on you; a label is distracting and unnecessary.

2. *Philosophy Statement.* Your beliefs about teaching and the process of learning will very likely enter into the selection process, but do not use résumé space for this purpose. A statement of your personal educational philosophy may be requested as a part of the application form or as a question during an interview.

3. *Personal Statement.* Your résumé is not the proper vehicle for conveying biographical details about your upbringing or your early educational experiences. Similarly, how you chose to pursue a teaching career, how you propose to conduct your classroom, or what you see yourself doing in the future are excellent topics for responses to open-ended questions on the application form or during the interview.

4. *Reason for Leaving Previous Position.* In a business résumé, it is sometimes considered possible to make a positive statement of professional growth by citing reasons for leaving a position. One can show a progression, indicate greater opportunity for responsibility or higher earnings, or promotion to a new project or level. This practice does not work for teachers, and there is no reason to attempt to define your career path in business terms. Educators work in a different environment and a different culture, and they define their achievements with a different vocabulary. They can change positions, change responsibilities, and change job titles, but the system does not allow for promotion.

5. *Availability*. There is no need to state that you will be available for a position beginning immediately or at a specified future date. Hiring officials will assume that you can begin when needed. Although emergencies or unforeseen circumstances can require immediate hiring, starting dates are not usually open to negotiation. The selection process is geared to the academic year or to the beginning of a semester or trimester.

6. *Date Prepared*. Your résumé will be considered current so long as it reflects your latest experiences. Assigning a date, however, can make it appear outdated within a few months even though nothing has changed. Let your cover letter serve to indicate the date your résumé was submitted.

7. *Ability to Travel or Relocate*. This is another carryover from the business world with little application to the field of education. Teachers might divide their responsibilities between schools in the same district, but overnight travel is simply not a factor for classroom teachers. A teacher may transfer from one building to another within a district, but because school districts are local entities, such transfer would rarely require changing one's residence.

8. *Salary*. Public school teachers generally do not have the opportunity to engage in individual negotiation for salary or benefits. A master contract governs placement on the salary scale, number of working days, holiday schedules, and conditions of employment. Salaries vary from district to district, from state to state, and from region to region. Whether your previous salary exceeds or falls short of the possibilities in the district to which you are applying is of no consequence; therefore, salary history has no place on your résumé.

NO APOLOGIES, NO EXCUSES

If you have gaps in your education or in your employment record, a history of job-hopping, even if you have been fired, you can stress the positive aspects of your experience. Pay special attention to how you organize this material. For example, if you have frequently moved from job to job, you won't want to emphasize dates of employment. They can be placed at the end of the entry, or even buried in the middle. You are not being deceptive; you are emphasizing the experience rather than the chronology.

If health problems caused an interruption in your career, the gap might be apparent to a careful reader, but you should not attempt to explain it. Any illness serious enough to cause a job interruption tends to frighten prospective employers. Save your explanation for the interview when you have the opportunity to demonstrate that you are physically capable of performing your duties and responsibilities.

Because you control the material presented in your résumé, you have the opportunity to present yourself in the best possible light. This does not mean you can be less than truthful. Every item on the résumé should work to your advantage: Stress the positives, avoid ambiguous or questionable entries, and weed out any item that could be construed as a negative. Accuracy and honesty are paramount, and misrepresentations, exaggerations, or actual lies are never acceptable.

As you begin to design your résumé, refer to the following model to remind you of what is included and what is omitted.

ADDRESS	(Include city, state, zip, phone, E-mail.)
RELEVANT EXPERIENCE	(List place, date, and brief description about field experiences, internships, practica, teaching assistantships, and student teaching experiences.)
RELATED ACTIVITIES	(Expand on projects or teaching-related activities, volunteer service, and community contributions.)
EMPLOYMENT	(List title of position, employer, location, and dates; briefly describe duties if related to teaching objective.)
ACTIVITIES AND DISTINCTIONS	(Include leadership positions, academic honors, and professional associations.)
EDUCATION	(State degrees held or in progress, certificates, licenses.)
INTERESTS	(Include academic, athletics, avocations.)
REFERENCES	(Indicate placement office, or state that references are available upon request.)

WHEN YOU PREPARE YOUR RESUME, REMEMBER–
- **NO** photograph
- **NO** personal information (age, sex, race, ethnicity, marital status)
- **NO** information about children, spouse, or significant other
- **NO** physical data (eye or hair color, weight, height)

5
ACTIVATE
YOUR RÉSUMÉ

The ability to write cohesive paragraphs using a balanced variety of simple, complex, and compound sentences is a decided asset. This skill, however, is not required in writing a résumé. You can appropriately demonstrate your mastery of the language in your cover letter and in other writing samples you may be asked to submit. At some point in the selection process, you will almost inevitably be asked to produce a short essay (often handwritten) describing your philosophy of education or your reasons for wanting to work in the district. Your résumé requires a different style of communication.

Active.

Quick.

Concise.

Convincing.

Action words and dynamic phrases create powerful impressions. Energize your activities, your skills, and your accomplishments with strong active language.

BE SELECTIVE

Avoid repetition; the impact of any word is diminished by too frequent use. Let's say you have developed five new instructional units that demonstrate your interest in several different curriculum areas. Your first draft might read like this:

Developed geography unit for third grade

Developed multigrade unit on the solar system

Developed...

Obviously, this leads to monotony. Almost any other approach would be better. An easy way to retain the impact of several similar activities without constant repetition might be to vary the wording and provide specifics:

Developed instructional units for various grade levels, including:

• Looking at Latitude and Longitude (Grade 4)

- Our Solar System (Grades 3–4)
- Fractions Are Fun (Grade 4)
- Alphabets and Hieroglyphics (Grade 3)
- Proper Nouns and Proper Caps (Grade 3)

USE ACTION WORDS

The following list of action words should help you get started. You can use some of these, or you can find other powerful verbs to create a dynamic picture of you and to suggest your potential.

Accomplish	Collect	Distribute
Achieve	Commended	Diversify
Acquired	Communicate	Document
Act	Compete	Draft
Adapt	Compile	Edit
Address	Complete	Educate
Adhere	Compose	Effect
Administer	Compute	Eliminate
Advance	Conceptualize	Enable
Advise	Conduct	Encounter
Analyze	Conserve	Encourage
Approve	Consolidate	Enlist
Arbitrate	Consult	Establish
Articulate	Contribute	Estimate
Ascertain	Control	Evaluate
Assemble	Coordinate	Examine
Assess	Correspond	Execute
Assist	Counsel	Expand
Attain	Create	Explain
Author	Critique	Extract
Balance	Cultivate	Facilitate
Budget	Define	Familiarize
Build	Deliver	Find
Calculate	Design	Focus
Catalog	Develop	Formulate
Chair	Devise	Furnish
Clarify	Diagnose	Gain
Classify	Direct	Generate
Coach	Discover	Group
Collaborate	Distinguish	Guide

Head	Organize	Rewarded
Host	Orient	Route
Identify	Originate	Schedule
Illustrate	Overhaul	Screen
Implement	Oversee	Secure
Improve	Participate	Select
Incorporate	Perform	Serve
Increase	Plan	Shape
Induce	Prepare	Skilled
Influence	Present	Solidify
Inform	Preside	Solve
Initiate	Prioritize	Specify
Innovate	Process	Sponsor
Install	Produce	Steer
Institute	Program	Stimulate
Integrate	Project	Streamline
Interpret	Promote	Strengthen
Interview	Provide	Study
Introduce	Publicize	Suggest
Invent	Publish	Summarize
Investigate	Quantify	Supervise
Involve	Received	Survey
Judge	Recommend	Systematize
Launch	Record	Target
Lead	Recruit	Teach
Lecture	Reduce	Test
Locate	Refer	Train
Maintain	Rehabilitate	Transform
Manage	Repair	Translate
Mediate	Replaced	Travel
Moderate	Represent	Trim
Monitor	Research	Upgrade
Motivate	Resolve	Utilize
Network	Restore	Validate
Nominated	Restructure	Venture
Nurture	Reverse	Verify
Observe	Review	Weigh
Obtain	Revise	Work
Operate	Revitalize	Write

Action words must be used accurately. Find a way to describe your role in any activity that neither overstates your case nor undervalues your achievement. If you chaired a committee, say so; just listing the name or function of the committee ignores your leadership role. On the other hand, if you were a member of a team that developed a new learning center, be careful about claiming all of the credit.

Discrepancies have a way of surfacing. Avoid placing yourself in a potentially awkward or embarrassing position.

SHORT PHRASES = EASY READING

One of the most effective methods of giving energy and life to your résumé is to make the writing flow easily and quickly. Complete sentences, however well constructed, cannot be read as quickly as fragments. Short phrases with strong verbs are easy to scan, conveying your message clearly and dynamically without verbal excess, redundant auxiliary verbs, or a clutter of personal pronouns. How long can anyone sustain interest when each sentence begins:

I was

I did

I have

I am

I made

I...

You get the idea. Sentence fragments allow you to skip over the repetitive personal pronoun and get directly to the important part, the activity or accomplishment, and to lead off each entry with a strong verb.

Suppose you found this on a résumé:

I have had the responsibility in April of each year for putting together the Washington School talent show, which earned money for the general fund.

Look at the difference when an action phrase replaces a complete sentence:

Created and organized profitable annual school talent show

By combining your activities with strong action verbs, the phrases on your résumé might look something like this:

- Utilized effective classroom management strategies

- Planned, prepared, and organized materials for thematic units

- Provided consistent enthusiasm and creativity in classroom activities

- Individualized instruction for students at all levels and abilities

- Facilitated the implementation of writing and reading strategies in ten elementary buildings

- Developed a training packet for portfolio assessment

- Instituted a new curriculum that included long-range plans to incorporate computer literacy into daily instruction

Action words and phrases in your résumé will produce a significant bonus. When you begin to interview for positions, you will already have the habit of expressing yourself in language that makes you sound vital, energetic, and enthusiastic.

CREATE YOUR OWN ACTION PHRASES

On the lines below, write action phrases that describe your skills, abilities, and accomplishments.

_____

_____

_____

_____

_____

_____

_____

_____

_____

CONSIDER PRIORITIES

As you incorporate these phrases into your résumé, try to match the significance of the item to its place on the page. Generally, you will want to lead with your strengths. The most important item should appear first.

PRODUCTION GUIDELINES

The most important feature of your résumé is what it says about you, but unless the overall appearance creates a good first impression, potential employers may not take time to examine the content. Imagine reading twenty résumés—or fifty, a hundred, a thousand, or more. Many hiring officials face exactly this task when they need to hire a teacher.

What can you do to make their job easier?

A hiring official responsible for reviewing application materials must look for quickly identifiable reasons to reject at least a portion of the applicants. Judging a résumé by its appearance requires comparatively little time or effort, and it is a standard and legitimate practice.

The old adage about not judging a book by its cover does not apply here. An unprofessional appearance makes a résumé easy to discard.

RÉSUMÉ LAYOUT

The arrangement of material on the page is referred to as the layout. The position and alignment of the information in the various sections of your résumé can make a vital difference in how you are perceived. Don't rush this stage of your résumé development. The samples in this book use several different layouts. Experiment with the effect of different layouts on your material. An effective layout guides the reader through the information about your education and experience, directing attention to your strengths while allowing the reader to assess your résumé easily and quickly.

Although there are no prescribed layouts for résumés, three styles are commonly used because they are easily prepared and professional in appearance.

Layout #1

This résumé is set up with a full block style. Every heading begins at the left margin, creating a sharp, clean look. Locations, dates, and other details about professional background are uniformly indented from the left. The shorter line necessitated by this style makes it especially appropriate if you have a limited amount of material.

J. J. CHRISTOPHERSEN

3 University Avenue, Any City, State 21345 (101) 555-0009
jjchristophersen@purdue.edu

OBJECTIVE

Japanese Language and Culture, grades 6 – 12
English as a Second Language, all levels

DEGREES

B.A. Degree, May 2004, Purdue University, West Lafayette, IN
Majors: Linguistics and Japanese with teacher licensure

INTERNSHIP

Japanese, grades 6 – 12, Bellton Academy, Chicago, Spring 2004
- Taught Japanese on four levels, including an Honors Class
- Assisted in the coordination of interdisciplinary projects with
  social studies classes and art classrooms
- Integrated technology into daily teaching with specialized software
- Developed alternative assessment methods including portfolios

ESL EXPERIENCE

English Teacher, Osaka Schools, Osaka, Japan, 2001 – 2003
- Team-taught, with Japanese mentor, English in three high schools
- Created daily lesson plans on grammar, spelling, and vocabulary
- Developed numerous supplementary teaching materials to use in the
  classroom and to share with students for nightly review
- Presented seminars and workshops to area teachers and participated
  in several cultural exchange programs

AFFILIATIONS

Indiana Second Language Educators
Association of Teachers of Japanese

PART-TIME WORK

Interpreter, Wong Travel Agency, Chicago, Summers 2003 – present
Tutor, Japanese language, private students, 2002 – present
Web page designer, Indiana Design Solutions, 2001 – 2002

REFERENCES

Available upon request.

Visit my Web site at *www.christophersen.portfolio.htm* to view
documentation of teaching skills, lesson planning, parent
communication, bilingual abilities, and assessment strategies.

Layout #2

This résumé uses centered section headings, and full margins for each entry. The wider line readily accommodates a larger volume of information. With appropriate indentation to allow for ample white space, the résumé can handle a longer text without resorting to dense blocks of print. It can also handle a shorter text if several indentations are made within entries or additional space separates each section.

TONY STEPHENS

3 University Avenue, Any City, State 21345   101.555.0009
tony-stephens@hotmail.com
www.tony.portfolio.education.asu.edu

COMPETENCIES AND INTERESTS

TEACHING COMPETENCIES
Computer-Aided Drafting
Technical Drawing
Architectural Instruction
Construction Technology

SPECIAL INTERESTS
Head Coach - Golf
Assistant Coach - Basketball
Sponsor - Robot Technology
Advisor - School Booster Club

ACADEMIC TRAINING

Arizona State University - Tempe, Bachelor of Science Degree, 1996, Computer Science
University of Oklahoma, Norman, Teaching License, May 2003, Industrial Technology

---

INTERNSHIP

H.S. Industrial Technology, **Flats High School, Norman, Oklahoma, Fall 2003**
- Taught computer-aided drafting and design classes to juniors and seniors
- Taught drafting exercises, including dimensioning, sectional views, pictorials, and architectural floor plan design; provided tutorial services for students seeking advanced training
- Planned and presented units on using hand tools and basic carpentry for a one-semester Home and Auto Repair course
- Evaluated student progress by using various assessment instruments including pretests, posttests, rubrics, and skills-based portfolios
- Integrated advanced technical applications into lessons and robotics activities
- Worked closely with local business and community leaders to raise funds for students to compete in regional robotic contests

---

UNIVERSITY ACTIVITIES AND AWARDS

University of Arizona Golf Team, 4 years; MVP, 2 years, All-Conference, 1 year
Performed in numerous volunteer fund-raising efforts for local charities
Arizona State Athletic Scholarship; Dean's List, 4 semesters; graduated with honors

---

PROFESSIONAL GOLF EXPERIENCE

Tour member, Western Golf Professional Tour, 1996 – 2001
- Traveled with tour and placed in the top 15; qualified for the U.S. Open, 1999

Credentials at Teacher Placement Center, Any City, State 21345   101.555.0008

30-->

Layout #3

This résumé style positions the section headings at the left margin, allowing a wide line for entries. Because the entire page can be used, it is a good choice if you need to include extensive descriptions or a number of different experiences. To use space effectively, the address is spread across the page directly below the name. A corresponding horizontal line at the bottom of the page gives it a finished appearance.

VERA GOODE

3 University Avenue, Any City, State 21345 (101) 555-0009
vera-goode@satuniv.edu

TEACHING SKILLS
Art Teacher – Middle School
- Special expertise in painting, sculpture, and multimedia
- Experience in designing integrated lessons in collaborative settings
- Technology skills in graphic design and various software applications

EDUCATION
B.F.A. Seattle University, May 2004
- International Study in Milan and Florence, Italy, 2002
- Kansas City Art Institute, 2001 – 2002

TEACHING INTERNSHIP
Art, Pacific Coast Middle School, Seattle, Spring 2004
- Teaching responsibilities included working with students in all classrooms, 5th – 8th grades
- Integrated lessons to reflect everyday activities and to include topics in science and social studies; lessons included bookmaking, painting, drawing, printmaking, weaving, metalworking and multimedia
- Created projects for all learners from inclusion students to non-English speakers
- Helped students display artwork in storefronts, local office buildings, and the Bay Museum

FIELD EXPERIENCE
Middle School and K-3 Art, Seattle Public Schools, Fall 2003
- Prepared lessons in ceramics, drawing, painting, calligraphy, puppet making, mixed media, and special research projects; organized several art shows and contests
- Guided an outdoor education art workshop for a team retreat
- Joined in child study teams and was available for after-school help on a daily basis

RECOGNITION
Academic
- Scholastic Art Award, Gold Key and Blue Ribbon
- Frank Jesper Scholarship

Art
- Group Show: Missouri Arts Show, Kansas City Art Center, 2003
- Juried Show: 40th Annual Seattle Artist's Show, Seattle, 2002
- Invitational Exhibition: Pacific Coast Invitational, Vancouver, 2001

PROFESSIONAL MATERIALS
Portfolio
- Web-based portfolio available for review or on-line at www.veragoode.education.htm

Recommendations
- Letters of reference at Education Placement Office, Any City, State 21345 (101) 555-0008

VISUAL FEATURES

Word processing or desktop publishing allows you to design a format that fits your needs and to select layout features to enhance your message. Variable sizes of print can make your résumé interesting and reader friendly as well as allow you to emphasize section headings, important assignments, or specific preparations. Scalable fonts available with personal computers make it possible to design an eye-catching résumé that subtly draws the reader's attention to the points you wish to highlight.

Don't get carried away with variety for variety's sake. Efficient communication depends on the twin goals of clarity and legibility. Unusual fonts such as "𝓸𝓵𝓭𝓮 𝓔𝓷𝓰𝓵𝓲𝓼𝓱" or *script* can be distracting, and even irritating. Keep your choices few, simple, and meaningful.

Hints:

- Nothing should be larger than your name.

- Section headings should be of uniform size.

- Annotations can appear less formidable and take up less of your valuable space if they use a slightly smaller font.

- Overuse of large print wastes space and time, because it slows the reader's eye, and may look like an attempt to stretch limited information.

WHITE SPACE

A judicious use of white space creates a layout that is both attractive and easy to read. White space makes your résumé far more inviting than a cramped, dense block of text bristling with dates and locations. Ample margins, extra spaces between sections, indentation, and the use of columns can all contribute to an airy and accessible effect.

ACCENTS AND EMPHASIS

Computer technology has made it very easy to add designs, figures, clip art, or drawings to a résumé. A note of caution regarding graphic enhancement is in order, however. Intricate patterns, cute figures, or large, bold designs appear gimmicky and draw attention away from the message of the résumé. In addition, if the potential employer's scanning technology does not readily accept graphics, the appearance and readability of your résumé is in jeopardy.

Design your résumé to direct the reader's attention to your strong points. Choose features that intensify the visual impact and improve the communication ability of your résumé. Simple techniques can achieve attractive and professional results. For example, a small bullet (•) or dash (–) can draw attention to a special item or unify similar entries:

- Elected student body president

- Nominated for Teacher of the Year

- Selected Rhodes Scholar regional finalist

Section headings can be accented with **bold** print or CAPITAL LET-TERS, making the divisions of your résumé more prominent. *Italic print* can be used for emphasis, or simply for variety. However, keep in mind that overuse of any of these accent techniques will diminish their effect.

7

THE FINAL PRODUCT

As you approach the final stages of résumé preparation, you must become not only a writer but also an editor. If you were writing for publication, you would have the luxury of working with an editor who could read your work with a clear and objective eye. The editor would catch inaccuracies and inconsistencies. Problems arising from ambiguities, extraneous language, and faulty organization would be spotted and resolved.

These editorial functions must be performed before your résumé is ready for production. If you are persuasive enough, you might talk someone else into editing your résumé for you. With or without assistance, you have ultimate responsibility for the final product. No one is in a better position to make editorial decisions about the relevance of each entry, the importance of individual word selection, and the effect created by the arrangement of the material.

Perhaps the most difficult aspect of editing your own material is deciding what to cut out. Everything you have put into your draft is there because it seems relevant. As a beginning teacher or a veteran with years of experience, you have to challenge the significance of each item, to question whether its contribution justifies the space it requires. Sometimes you can compromise; sometimes you simply have to be ruthless in your actions.

PROOFREADING

After you have drafted, revised, and edited your résumé, there is one more step before you are ready to produce the genuine article. That important step is proofreading. Never neglect or underestimate the importance of proofreading.

One simple mistake can be disastrous. Take the time to check each word for spelling and each entry for accuracy, grammar, and punctuation. Make full use of a computer's spell-checker if you can, but don't rely on it completely. It won't recognize a misplaced or misused word if it is spelled correctly.

You have the ultimate responsibility for the document, but you probably will not be the best proofreader. After you have written, rewritten, chopped, added, cut and pasted, thrown it away and started over, you will very likely see what you expect to see. Get help from friends, colleagues, roommates, instructors—anyone who is willing and reasonably knowledgeable—even Uncle Jack. Make any necessary changes or corrections, and then move into the production stage.

PRODUCTION

The availability of campus computer systems and of personal computers has made dramatic changes in the way most résumés are produced. Tailoring a résumé to meet the requirements of a specific job, rearranging categories to highlight particularly appropriate skills or experiences, or simply updating and changing an address is quickly and easily accomplished

Print Quality. Any printer can give you a draft version so you can begin to see how your résumé will look. For the final version, only a clear, sharp image is acceptable. Most printers can give you a finished copy that represents you as a professional.

Special Note: Professional papers are not handwritten. You may have the most sophisticated handwriting, you may print beautifully, or you may even be a master of calligraphy, but your résumé is not the place to demonstrate these abilities. It is also unprofessional and inadvisable to make handwritten corrections, additions, or updates to a conventionally produced résumé.

MULTIPLE PAGES

If your résumé consists of more than one page, each page after the first should be numbered. Your name should appear on every page. Do not fasten the pages together with staples or clips and never print on both sides of the page.

Presentations on 11 × 17-inch paper, folded in half to create a brochure effect, are difficult to scan or to copy. Because they require a minimum of two full pages of text, they are unsuitable for nearly all beginning teachers, who may attempt to fill a brochure with large fonts, extra spacing, or extraneous descriptions. Even for experienced professionals, the brochure offers no clear advantage.

PAPER SELECTION

The paper you select for your résumé contributes to your professional image. It does not have to be the most expensive stock available, but it should be at least 20-pound bond. Standard size for a professional resume is $8^{1}/_{2}$ × 11 inches. Larger or smaller paper is usually more of a nuisance than an asset; it doesn't stack or file properly, and it cannot be copied as readily.

The exact weight or texture of the paper you select is a matter of personal taste, but anything truly unusual should be avoided. Similarly, the use of colored stock is a legitimate option. Soft tints in neutral colors are acceptable and can be attractive. Bright colors will, indeed, attract attention, but perhaps not the kind of attention you want to receive. Plain white paper is always a viable option for creating a crisp, professional image.

Using the same paper for your correspondence with employers is a good idea. Matching envelopes are a nice added touch, though the envelope is often discarded immediately upon opening.

THE FINAL REVIEW

Never submit a résumé that does not represent your best interests. Any of the following flaws could be fatal to your chances:

- Lack of focus or direction
- Long, rambling sentences
- Overuse of personal pronoun
- Dense blocks of narrative
- Poor print quality (light, faded)
- Inconsistent format

Anything less than perfection will detract from your overall impression. Evidence of carelessness in producing or handling the document—any smudge, stain, dog-eared corner, or unnecessary crease or fold—is grounds for immediate rejection.

A good-looking résumé will get you noticed; you get only one chance to make a good impression.

ELECTRONIC RÉSUMÉS

Without a doubt, electronic résumés are playing an increasingly important role in the marketplace. Cyberspace provides today's educators new opportunities and new avenues to conduct a job search. A résumé created on your computer can be attached to an e-mail document, uploaded to a web-based résumé service or, perhaps, to a school district's on-line application form. Because some graphic features (underlining, bullets, symbols, bold) may not be recognized, your electronic résumé should employ simple means of emphasis.

YOUR RÉSUMÉ AND THE WORLD WIDE WEB

The Internet and the World Wide Web present yet another marketing opportunity for educators seeking new positions. Designing an on-line résumé demands the same careful attention to relevance and professionalism as a conventional résumé.

The most effective Web résumé presents your skills, abilities, and training unencumbered by extraneous material.

- Never provide personal data or photographs to potential employers.
- Avoid informal chat or lingo.
- Resist dark or heavily patterned backgrounds.
- Using clip art is unoriginal and unnecessary. "Borrowing" cartoons or other copyrighted material is unprofessional and illegal.
- Provide links only to your E-mail address and to your electronic portfolio containing material you have created, e.g., lesson plans, philosophy statement, management strategies.

Consider your Web résumé a supplement to the résumé you have already created for paper or E-mail submission. It need not be a replica of your initial résumé. You can expand on some categories and minimize others and you can provide a link to your own electronic portfolio.

A well-prepared electronic portfolio offers opportunities to incorporate features not available in any other format. Images, sounds, video, and links to other Web sites can all be brought into your electronic portfolio, demonstrating your technology skills and your creativity as well as your knowledge of curriculum and pedagogy. Effective portfolios present your skills, abilities, and training unencumbered by extraneous material.

Put your address of your Web site or URL (Uniform Resource Locator) on the résumé you use to introduce yourself to potential employers. Your URL can appear with your address at the top of the paper résumé or at the bottom of your E-mail version.

SURVIVING THE SCANNER

Scanning technology used for recruitment and screening purposes, however, sophisticated, has two simple purposes: to enter your résumé into a database and to sort for keywords significant to the employer. School districts may have any number of terms entered into their database, and the keywords they use are determined by their needs, their philosophies, their educational goals, and the demographics of the community.

Provide clear and specific information about your skills and experiences. For example, if you describe yourself as bilingual, you may increase your chances of being selected by the scanner if you add qualifiers such as "bilingual—Spanish/English" or "bilingual—Hmong and English."

Scanning software does not read graphics, including diamonds, bullets, check marks, horizontal or vertical lines, or text boxes. Scanners read standard fonts such as Courier or Helvetica without difficulty, but may not recognize other font styles.

Textured or colored paper stock is also problematic. To be on the safe side, use ordinary white paper, a standard font, black print, and no graphics. This plain, ungarnished document may not have the visual interest of your paper résumé, but it will survive the scanner and allow you to be considered for available positions.

EMPLOYER EXPECTATIONS ABOUT RÉSUMÉS

Whether they are holding your résumé in their hand or reading it on a computer screen, hiring officials have a limited amount of time to make preliminary or first-round selections. Screening can be based solely on a quick glance at your résumé and cover letter. It doesn't take long to make decisions—maybe thirty seconds, maybe even less. Surprising as it may seem, your résumé and your future can be relegated to a stack labeled *Yes*, *No*, or *Maybe* on the basis of a rapidly formed opinion.

Very few principals or superintendents would consider themselves experts in the art of constructing a résumé. In the limited amount of time they can devote to the screening process, they make quick, hard decisions based on the following simple criteria:

- Neat, fresh, legible, and error-free résumé
- Clearly identified teaching field, skills, strengths
- Effective language and correct grammar
- Positive and promising professional image

Surviving this initial screening is critical but it is not particularly difficult. Avoiding the *No* bin, the wastebasket, or the Delete key demands that your paper or electronic image be convincing, relevant, and positive.

TAILORING YOUR RÉSUMÉ

A résumé should be designed to accomplish a specific purpose; in other words, your résumé must fit the job. Tailoring a résumé for specific jobs can be easily accomplished. By rearranging categories, highlighting the most relevant experiences or qualifications, adding or deleting details, you can target a specific job. Personal computers make this a simple task.

For example, if you are certified to teach social studies, you will probably start with a résumé that presents your qualifications as a generalist. As opportunities arise, modifications can be made to reflect your preparation in such specific areas as American history, government, world history, or international affairs.

A music teacher, for example, may be licensed to work with students from kindergarten through 12th grade in general and vocal music. One résumé could emphasize preparation and experience for working with high school choral groups; another version could concentrate on a general music program for elementary students.

A RÉSUMÉ IS NOT AN ALL-PURPOSE DOCUMENT

Your employment résumé addresses skills, strengths, competencies, extracurricular interests, and educational background. If you are seeking two distinctly different kinds of positions, such as classroom teacher and school principal, you need to prepare more than one résumé. Obviously, these positions have different responsibilities; they require different preparations and different skills. A teaching résumé, however well prepared, will send the wrong message in an administrative search: it could imply that you are insufficiently aware of the differences between teaching and administration, that you have not given enough thought to changing jobs, or that you are simply a poor communicator.

RÉSUMÉS FOR OTHER PURPOSES

Perhaps the most widely recognized use of a résumé is in the employment process, but educators will find many other situations in which a résumé can be a useful tool:

- Evaluations/performance reviews

40

- Grant proposals
- Applications for special honors, awards
- Conference presentations
- Candidacy for election to office in a professional association
- Background material for the person who introduces you as a speaker or panel member

A résumé used for general introductions presents experiences, leadership roles, recognitions, and other accomplishments selected and arranged for their relevance. For example, if you are to present a paper or a talk at a professional conference, you might be asked to provide background information to the person who will introduce you. You would prepare a different résumé for the person who will introduce your address to a local service club. See examples on pages 150 and 172.

Similarly, you might find it necessary to prepare a résumé for a performance review or evaluation, to accompany a grant application, or to provide information when you are a candidate for office in a professional association. A résumé can also be helpful in support of your nomination or application for an award. Each of these occasions requires a customized résumé that could be quite different from the résumé sent to a potential employer. The content, the arrangement, and the emphasis must be directed toward the proper goal.

Note: Shortcuts won't work. Take time to prepare different versions. Your résumé must be appropriate for the purpose.

10
RÉSUMÉS FOR ADMINISTRATORS

Candidates for an administrative position at the building or central office level need to craft a résumé specifically targeted for the available position, carefully outlining educational training, specific skills, and accumulated experiences. The most effective résumés for educators in administrative or supervisory roles focus on competencies and experiences directly related to immediate objectives.

In current practice, an administrator's résumé will be carefully reviewed by many different people involved in the selection process, from school board officials to community representatives. Acronyms, abbreviations, technical terminology, and currently fashionable catchwords should be avoided or used sparingly. The content of your résumé must be comprehensible to people who are not trained educators, yet sufficiently detailed to be meaningful to practicing professionals.

NEW ADMINISTRATORS

A teacher seeking an entry-level administrative position must demonstrate successful teaching experiences as well as leadership capabilities and responsibilities assumed in school or community projects. Service or leadership at the department, building, or district level illustrates interest, commitment, and involvement.

Key items for a new administrator's résumé:

- Evidence of academic training in educational administration

- Identified professional strengths and abilities

- Documented experience as a successful teacher

- Manifest commitment to students, colleagues, and the learning community

EXPERIENCED ADMINISTRATORS

If you are a veteran administrator, a complete list of your activities and responsibilities over the years could produce a document running to several single-spaced pages. For maximum impact, priorities must be assigned in order to trim your résumé to a manageable size. Editing—selecting, summarizing, and condensing your career experiences and achievements into an effective promotional package—could be your most difficult task.

In addition to an employment history, experienced administrators should provide evidence of current and continuing development. Membership in professional associations is expected; presentations, recognitions, or positions of responsibility at the local, regional, or national level should be highlighted.

Key items for experienced administrators are:

- Evidence of building staff and community consensus in support of district goals
- Management skills in finance, enrollment, and diversity issues
- Proficiency in administrative and instructional technology
- Exemplary leadership in curriculum and commitment to academic success for all students

An effective way to demonstrate your past achievements is to design a résumé section or even a special page entitled Professional Activities and Accomplishments. Topics to consider including are:

- Curriculum Development
- Committee Leadership
- Strategic Planning
- Staff Development and In-service
- Financial Management
- Policy Development
- District Initiatives
- Grant Writing
- Building Referendums
- Selected Presentations
- Professional/Community Service

VERONICA KIRKWOOD

PROFESSIONAL ACTIVITIES AND ACCOMPLISHMENTS

SERVICE AND LEADERSHIP
Committee participation
- Cochair, Graduate Student Advisory Committee, 2003 – present
- Graduate Student Representative, Five-year Program Review, 2003
- Chair, English Language Development Committee, 2002 – 2003
- Vice-Chair, Bilingual Curriculum Committee, 2001 – 2002
- Member, Student Attendance Review Board, 1999
- Member, Multicultural Curriculum Review Committee, 1999
- Member, Student Study Team, 1998
- Leadership Team Member, Program Quality Review, 1996 – 1998

In-service presentations
- "Monolingual Teachers and Bilingual Students: How Can We Communicate?"
- "Cooperative Learning Projects in the Bilingual Classroom"
- "Understanding Cultural Differences and the English as a Second Language Student"

Special projects
- Desert Cities Regional Reading Council
- Strategic Planning Board for Alvord United School District
- Community Parent Outreach Project
- School/Business Alliance of Riverside County

Recent conferences
- Annual Meeting of the National Association of Elementary School Principals, Orlando, Florida, March 2003
- Association of Overseas Educators, Indiana, Pennsylvania, Fall 2000
- Western Regional Meeting of Bilingual Educators, Provo, Utah, Spring 1999

SPECIAL RECOGNITION
Distinguished Teacher of the Year Award, California State University
University Graduate Thesis Award for Outstanding Research
Graduate Leadership Award, College of Education, University of Southern California
Undergraduate Achievement Scholarship, California State University

AFFILIATIONS
National Association of Secondary School Principals
Association of Overseas Educators
Association for Supervision and Curriculum Development
California Women in Educational Leadership

PROFESSIONAL DOCUMENTS
Dossier: Career Center, Any City, State 21345   101.555.0011
Portfolio: Standards-based online portfolio at: www.portfolio.veronicakirkwood.usc.htm

An overview of professional experience at the beginning of the résumé can be particularly helpful to the reader. It provides a quick summary of your career progression and establishes a framework for the entire presentation.

- Assistant Superintendent   3 years
- High School Principal   6 years
- Assistant Principal   2 years
- Classroom Teacher   5 years

For administrators at any level, accuracy is paramount; any error, inconsistency, or misrepresentation will prove damaging if not fatal. An attractive, purposeful résumé will enhance your image as a dynamic, knowledgeable leader.

11

RÉSUMÉS FOR INTERNATIONAL TEACHING

A specialized résumé will be essential if you are seeking a teaching position in another country. International schools are looking for people who are flexible, adaptable, and independent. A résumé that reflects these essential qualities, and portrays you as a versatile educator who can contribute to several different areas of school life will immediately catch the international employer's attention.

Tailor your international résumé carefully, and consider it a single-purpose document. There are a few adjustments you will need to make on a résumé that is designed solely for international opportunities. In addition to presenting your credentials, focus on skills and attributes that have special significance for international hiring officials.

GENUINE RÉSUMÉ ASSETS

Foreign Language Ability
In American-sponsored international schools, the language of instruction will be English. You need not be fluent in the language of the host country to be considered for employment. However, knowledge of any foreign language will contribute to your ability to learn the language of your new community and will make for an easier transition.

International Experience
Previous experience of living and/or studying in another country will be viewed positively by prospective employers. If you spent a summer, a semester, or an academic year abroad, be sure to include all relevant information. Exchange students who have the advantage of living with a host family may have an easier adjustment to living in a new setting.

Travel
Experienced travelers are more likely to adjust quickly to a new setting. Even a limited exposure to different cultures, new surroundings, and unfamiliar customs will usually lessen the severity and shorten the duration of the inevitable culture shock.

Related Interests

A demonstrated commitment to learning about other cultures and a concern for international affairs can be displayed on your résumé by stating membership in various kinds of international clubs or associations, volunteer service as a guide, language partner, or "friend" to foreign students, or even by elective courses in relevant ethnic, cultural, or area studies.

Other Interests

Leisure time can pose problems for people who depend on activities or resources not universally available. Avocations (photography, philately, sketching, reading, needlework, writing, hiking, and sightseeing) that can be pursued independently and without group or family support provide yet another indication of probable success in adjusting to a strange environment.

CITIZENSHIP AND OTHER DATA

A special section of your résumé should be devoted to personal information including citizenship, marital status, and number of dependents who would accompany you. It is not necessary to include vital statistics (age, height, weight, religion, or ethnic identity). (See résumés in the International Settings section, beginning on page 163.) Unlike stateside hiring officials, directors of international schools may have a genuine need to be aware of your marital status and number of dependents. In some locations, housing suitable for families is simply not available. Only single teachers or a teaching couple with no dependent children can be considered for employment. The extreme difficulty or sheer impossibility of obtaining a work permit for a nonteaching spouse can also make it necessary for employers to hire only teaching couples or single teachers.

12

RÉSUMÉS FOR SECOND CAREER AND NONLICENSED INDIVIDUALS

The demand for new teachers in shortage areas and attempts to increase the diversity of classroom teachers by attracting career changers and members of under-represented racial and ethnic groups have contributed to the growth of alternative certification programs. Some alternative certification programs seek to recruit mature individuals who retire from or wish to leave a successful career to pursue an interest in teaching. Programs such as Troops to Teachers have been developed to encourage military personnel nearing retirement from active duty to enter the teaching profession.

A number of states have implemented alternative routes to certification for college graduates who lack practicum experiences or course work in pedagogy prescribed for state-approved teacher preparation programs. Some states issue provisional teaching licenses only in areas where there is a severe shortage of licensed teachers, whereas other states offer provisional certificates and alternative certification programs in any teaching field.

Some alternative certification programs have been developed by individual school districts; for example, the Los Angeles Unified School District's internship program trains about three hundred teachers a year. Agreements between individual school districts and the state department of education may permit schools to hire college graduates who then work to obtain licensure for that district only.

According to federal and state employment reports, the overall job market for teachers is expected to provide many job opportunities through at least the first decade of the twenty-first century. In practice, however, opportunities for teachers vary widely by location and by teaching field. State-mandated reductions in class size, increased enrollments, and the anticipated retirement of large numbers of teachers combine to create local and regional shortages of qualified educators. Even without a teaching license, it is possible to explore employment opportunities in schools and other educational settings.

Public Schools

Although most public schools require a teaching license, in some locations (both urban and rural) and in some teaching fields, college graduates can be employed as teachers with provisional licenses, usually with the expectation that license requirements will be met. School district Web sites often include information about opportunities for both licensed and nonlicensed employment.

Independent Schools

Some states do not require state certification for teachers in nonpublic or independent schools, a classification that can include preparatory schools, boarding schools, and parochial schools. Independent schools may offer internship or teaching fellowship opportunities for first-year teachers. Typically, a fellowship provides a stipend rather than a full salary.

English Language Instruction

Language centers around the world employ native speakers as instructors of conversational English. Major corporations and educational institutions in South America, Africa, Asia, and Eastern Europe hire college graduates interested in living and teaching in a different environment and culture. Teaching experience and certification are not required. Although advertisements frequently refer to ESL, TOEFL, or TESOL, teaching positions may not require specific training in English or linguistics.

Preschools

Preschool and day-care centers afford opportunities for college students and for college graduates who are interested in working with young children. Teaching certificates are not typically required, although some states license head teachers or directors of day-care centers.

Learning Centers and Agencies

Private agencies provide tutoring and special assistance to students at various levels, from young children to adult learners. Depending on the center's philosophy or mission, the instruction may be geared toward developmental or accelerated learning. These agencies hire both certified teachers and noncertified teachers with a strong academic background in the tutorial area.

Health Care Facilities

Educational departments or divisions for pediatric patients exist in nearly all major hospitals. Individuals work with long-term patients or homebound students in virtually all subject areas. Some opportunities exist for instructors or tutors who are not licensed teachers.

RELEVANT HIGHLIGHTS

Information about preprofessional activities, such as student teaching or practicum experiences, is an important résumé section for licensed teachers. Noncertified teachers must concentrate on other experiences that highlight related background, appropriate skills, and demonstrated abilities.

Special attention must be given to selecting, assigning priorities, and arranging résumé items. The same person could conceivably prepare a résumé for teaching either in a preschool or a college preparatory school. Much of the information would be the same; however, sections of the résumé could be modified to emphasize different skills and experiences.

- Experience with appropriate age-groups
- Volunteer activities
- Personal attributes
- Relevant course work
- Special skills, competencies
- Cultural awareness
- Travel
- Language skills
- Involvement/Activism
- Leadership

13
EFFECTIVE COVER LETTERS

Even the greatest soloist usually requires an accompanist. Your best résumé, too, will need a companion piece—usually called a cover letter.

Writing a good basic cover letter is much easier than preparing a résumé. You have fewer choices to worry about; there are simple conventions for standard business letters, and you should follow them.

For cover letters submitted by conventional means (on paper and delivered by mail):

- Use standard 8½ × 11-inch stationery, preferably the same paper stock you have chosen for your résumé.

- Use only one side of the page.

- The return address and the date should appear at the top of the page.

- The inside address (name and title of the individual, name and address of the institution) should appear at least three spaces below the date and flush with the left margin.

- The body of the letter should be single-spaced, with double spacing between paragraphs.

- Paragraphs may begin at the left margin or a half-inch to the right.

- The complimentary close should appear two spaces below the last line of the letter.

- Leave four spaces between the complimentary close and your name to allow for your signature.

- The word "enclosure" appears two or more spaces below your name when you include additional items, for example, résumé, transcripts, application form.

BEYOND THE MECHANICS—OR, WHAT DO I WRITE?

Start at the beginning. You cannot go wrong by clearly stating the purpose of your letter in your opening sentence—or at least early in the first paragraph. Because many school districts have a number of positions available, a clear statement of why you are writing will allow the employer to process your application efficiently.

Once the opening lines are out of the way, go on to the main idea. In a letter of application for employment, this means pointing out specific qualifications and experiences directly related to the available position. Highlight relevant experiences, emphasize appropriate training, and sell yourself as a competent and committed professional. This middle section or the concluding paragraph of your letter can provide information about supporting documents such as references or transcripts.

A letter of application should always include some reference to the next step in the process—the interview. You may request an appointment directly or use a slightly more subtle phrase such as, "I am very interested in this position and look forward to discussing it with you," but let the reader know that you want to arrange an interview.

Outside of education, job seekers are encouraged to be direct and assertive about the next step. Frequently, a letter concludes with a statement such as, "I will call you next Thursday to arrange an interview." This approach may work in some business fields, but it is not appropriate for educators. Because selection processes in education involve extensive paper screening, employers will initiate the arrangements for interviews.

COMMUNICATION IS THE GOAL

The ability to write clear, elegant prose is certainly an asset, but you don't have to be a great writer to produce a good letter. And you don't have to get writer's block when you sit down to compose a cover letter.

Complete sentences grouped in cohesive paragraphs are all that is required. Pay careful attention to spelling, grammar, and punctuation. Keep your language professional; resist any temptation to inflate your vocabulary in order to sound more intellectual or knowledgeable. No literary prizes are at stake; all you need to do is convey your message clearly and correctly.

SAMPLE COVER LETTER

221 College Street
Any City, State 12345
March 28, 2003

Lee Smith, Ph.D.
Superintendent
Anyplace School District
City, State 12347

Dear Dr. Smith:

Please consider me as an applicant for the high school language arts opening currently being advertised by Anyplace School District. I recently learned of your teaching opening from the Educational Placement Office at Central State University where I will earn my bachelor's degree in May of this year with a major in English and a minor in journalism and mass communication.

As the enclosed résumé indicates, I am completing a full semester internship at City High School working with a diverse student population in grades nine through twelve. In addition to my classroom experiences teaching British Literature, Twentieth-Century American Authors, and ninth grade Basic English, I volunteer to work individually and in small groups with the school's newspaper staff. I am particularly interested in your advertised opening because of the specific teaching responsibilities and the opportunity to serve as advisor to the student magazine and work with other student publications.

As your advertisement instructs, I have completed the school district's on-line application and am currently arranging for Central University's Registrar's Office to submit my transcripts to you. My letters of recommendation are being sent from the Educational Placement Office. I would welcome the opportunity to interview with your selection team, and I look forward to hearing from you in the near future.

Sincerely,

Ima Sample

Enclosure

PART TWO

SAMPLE RÉSUMÉS

14

MAKING THE BEST USE OF THESE SAMPLES

If you do nothing more than flip through the following samples, find the one that most closely matches your teaching area, and plug in your own information, you'll have an acceptable résumé. It might even look as good as most of the others in the stack on the employer's desk.

But it won't be the best résumé you could create. Remember, you don't have to settle for just a satisfactory appearance. Your résumé can do more than merely convey information to someone else; it can help you identify and concentrate on your particular strengths and interests, and organize your thoughts in preparation for interviews.

Take the time to read Part I of this book so you will understand how to capitalize on your strengths and abilities and how to convey these strengths and abilities to potential employers. Once you have read the introductory material, you will see how the samples work. You will understand how to highlight a special skill, how to emphasize a particular experience, and how to minimize events or circumstances that could be perceived as liabilities.

The sample résumés represent a wide variety of teaching interests, fields, specializations, and experiences. It would be natural to start with the one that seems to be the closest match. Before you adopt this résumé as your model, however, look at several others. You may find one in a different teaching field that is better suited to your particular situation.

Don't hesitate to combine elements of different samples. You might choose the layout from one, the category headings from another (with your own modifications), the font or typeface from a third, a graphic from yet another. You can borrow, incorporate, or adapt from any number of samples to create your personal résumé.

Add your own touches as well. The final product will represent you as a distinctive individual:

- an educator with an awareness of teaching capabilities and special strengths;

- an educator with recognized talents and accomplishments; and

- an educator who demonstrates personal commitment and professional purpose.

15

BEGINNING TEACHERS

ROCCO CASEY SAMUELS

3 University Avenue, Any City, State 21345   101.555-0009
rocco-sam@und.nodak.edu

TEACHING INTERESTS

Teacher: Early Childhood Education; Preschool Education

DEGREES

University of North Dakota, Grand Forks
M.A. Degree – May 2005   Early Childhood
B.A. Degree – May 2002   Majors: Early Childhood Education; Elementary Education

COURSE HIGHLIGHTS

Educational Psychology	Early Childhood Teaching	Language and Society
Multicultural-Bilingual Education	Child Development	Spanish I–IV
Early Language and Literacy	Classroom Management	Classroom Technology

STUDENT TEACHING

Early Childhood Center, University Center, Grand Forks, Fall 2004
Responsibilities:
• Instructed a diverse student population including English-as-a-Second-Language students
• Organized and created learning centers and bulletin boards
• Used cooperative learning strategies
• Introduced computer use in learning centers
• Provided students with individualized attention
• Created flannel-board stories to enhance learning
• Kept concise records of students' progress
• Worked productively with staff, students, and parents

Kindergarten, Pierce Elementary, Grand Forks, Fall 2003
Responsibilities:
• Developed learning stations in reading and science
• Taught reading to a small group of beginning readers
• Designed and maintained progress charts
• Communicated with parents on a regular basis sending newsletters and E-mails
• Attended Child Study team meetings and staffing meetings for learning disabled

RELATED ACTIVITIES

Member, National Association for Young Children (NAYC), 2003 – present
Attended, National Conference, NAYC, Chicago, Spring 2003
Hospital tutor, University of North Dakota Medical Center, summers 2000 – present
Crisis volunteer, Community Center, Grand Forks, 2002 – 2004

Credentials: Career Planning and Placement, Any City, State 21345   101.555.0008
On-line portfolio: www.rocco-sams.education/portfolio   Paper portfolio: available upon request

HILLARY CAPOUCHE

3 University Avenue, Any City, State 21345   (101) 555-0009
hillary-capouche@vsu.edu

OBJECTIVE   Bilingual Kindergarten Teacher

SKILLS

Multicultural teaching experience
Fluent in Spanish
Trained in early childhood developmental philosophy
Understand the educational needs of at-risk students

EDUCATIONAL BACKGROUND

Bachelor of Arts Degree, May 2004   Virginia Tech, Blacksburg, Virginia
Major: Early Childhood; Minor: English as a Second Language

University of Puerto Rico-Bayamon Campus, Bayamon, Puerto Rico 2002

INTERNSHIP EXPERIENCE

Transitional Kindergarten Intern, Community Schools of Blacksburg

Responsibilities in the five-month, Spring 2004 internship include:
• Develop and conduct classroom lessons in both Spanish and English
• Reinforce material by involving non–English speaking parents in the classroom and school activities
• Write and implement individualized education plans for each student and review with parents in school or home-based conferences
• Work extensively with individual students in beginning reading program
• Use cultural activities, songs, and materials to enhance learning and self-esteem

CLASSROOM EXPERIENCES

Bilingual Kindergarten Practicum, Fall 2003
First Grade Reading Recovery Program Observation, Summer 2003
Transitional First Grade Practicum, Spring 2003

TECHNOLOGY

Web management skills; digital audio and video; software design
View web site at: www.hcapouche.vt.edu

SERVICE

Habitat for Humanity Volunteer, Norfolk, Virginia, Summers, 2001– present
• Work with student and adult volunteers from various parts of the country to rebuild homes for families in need.

COLLEGE ACTIVITIES

Board Member, Student Activities Council
Player/coach, Intramural Basketball; volunteer referee
Team leader, Virginia River Festival

CREDENTIALS   Education Career Office, Any City, State 21345 (101) 555-0008

CALLIE CRAWFORD
3 University Avenue   Any City, State 21345   101.555.1111   c-crawford@nau.edu

ACADEMIC INTERESTS AND TRAINING
Teaching Interests
Elementary Education: Interested in integrative approach to lesson design
and extensive collaboration with teaching teams, parents, support staff, and administrators

Degrees
M.A.   Elementary Education, Curriculum Emphasis, Northern Arizona University, June 2004
       Teacher Certification Program, K-8
B.S.   Marketing, University of Arizona, Tucson, Arizona, May 2000

GRADUATE COURSES OF INTEREST
Curriculum Foundations   Educational Measurement
Reading and Writing Across Intermediate Grades The Adolescent and Young Adult
Construction and Use of Evaluation Instruments Technology in the Classroom

CLASSROOM EXPERIENCE
Graduate Internship: Fifth/Sixth Grade, Roosevelt Elementary Learning Center, Flagstaff, Fall 2003
- Used various teaching and management strategies—including cooperative learning, hands-on
  approaches, and interdisciplinary activities—to meet the learning needs of a multicultural class
- Worked extensively with mentor teacher on integrated lesson planning, assessment strategies
  (rubrics, portfolios, conferencing, examinations), and parent communication
- Developed and taught an integrated unit about ecology, which included a service-learning project
- Worked closely with teaching team, counselor, special education consultants, and administrators
  to identify students' learning difficulties and develop appropriate learning strategies and materials

Methods Practicum: Third/Fourth Grade, East Elementary, Flagstaff, Spring 2003
- Taught math and science to students in a mixed ability classroom using various motivational strategies
  to reach all learners; organized hands-on science units with field trips, labs, and projects
- Used traditional methods and technology tools, including various computer software programs and
  appropriate Internet sites, to reinforce abstract mathematical concepts

AFFILIATIONS AND ACTIVITIES
International Reading Association; Arizona Area Reading Council; Phi Delta Kappa
Math and Science Tutor, Flagstaff Children's Resource Center, 2003 – present
Special Olympics Volunteer, Flagstaff and Northern Arizona Council, 2003 – present

PROFESSIONAL EMPLOYMENT
Marketing Specialist: Towers, Mac and Associates, Phoenix, Arizona, June 2000 – August 2002
- Worked on special accounts for the advertising unit with clients on the West Coast

REFERENCES: Career Center, Any City, State 21345 (101) 555-0008

PORTFOLIO: To view integrated lesson planning, assessment strategies, beliefs, and parent
communication go to: *www.callie-crawford.education.una.btm*

LUCY SAMS

3 University Avenue • Any City, State 21345 • (101) 555-0008 • lucy-sams@uic.edu

OBJECTIVE AND SKILLS

Teacher: Intermediate Grades
Skills: Integrative Approach to Lesson Design
             Emphasis Multiculturalism in the Classroom
             Create Authentic Learning Experiences
             Collaboration with Teaching Teams, Administration, and Parents

ACADEMIC BACKGROUND

University of Illinois - Chicago   August 2000 – May 2004
- B.A. Degree, Elementary Education, Specialization in Science and Social Studies
  Order of Omega National Greek Honor Society
  University of Illinois Honors Program and Dean's List

STUDENT TEACHING

Intermediate Team, Belmont Elementary, Chicago Public Schools, Spring 2004
- Used various teaching and management strategies including cooperative learning, hands-on approaches to learning, and interdisciplinary activities
- Developed and taught an integrated theme on Plants and Seeds, which infused all subject areas with a literature-based approach
- Planned, prepared, and organized materials for thematic units on cities and measurement
- Integrated computer technology into daily classroom activities
- Taught science and bridged the concrete to the abstract through the use of manipulatives and computer activities

PRACTICA

Field Experience in Third through Sixth Grade Units and Classes, 2001 – 2003
- Intermediate Unit – Science and Math, Wicks Elementary, Fall 2003, Chicago
- Fifth/Sixth Grade – Social Studies, Mann Elementary, Spring 2002, Evanston
- Third/Fourth Grade – All subjects, Hoover Elementary, Fall 2001, Chicago

RELATED ACTIVITIES

Volunteer and Part-time Work Experience, 2000 – present
- Reading Volunteer, William Taylor Elementary, 2003 – present, Chicago
- Participant, Project Learning Tree Workshop, March 2003, Chicago
- Camp Counselor, YMCA Camp of the Rockies, Summers 2000 – 2002, Boulder, Colorado

CAMPUS INVOLVEMENT

Residence Hall Floor Government and Leadership, 2001 – 2004
- Floor President, 2003 – 2004
- Member of Alpha Delta Pi Sorority, Corresponding Secretary, 2001 – present
- Member of Student Alumni Ambassadors, 2001 – present

References at Educational Placement Office, Any City, State 21345 (101) 555-0008
Electronic Teaching Portfolio at *www.lucysams.ed.uillinois.htm*

JILL W. JEFFERSON

3 University Avenue, Any City, State 21345   (101)555-0009   jill-jefferson@du.edu

TEACHING INTERESTS AND SKILLS

Teacher: Multiage, Multilevel Elementary Education (K-8)
Special skills: collaborative planning, team teaching, inclusion, proactive management

ACADEMIC BACKGROUND

Bachelor of Arts Degree, *with honors,* University of Denver, July 2004
Major: Elementary Education; Area of Specialization: English/Language Arts and Technology
Presidential Honors Citation   Dean's List   Academic Achievement Award

STUDENT TEACHING INTERNSHIP EXPERIENCE

Multilevel grades, Colorado Middle School, Denver Public Schools, Spring 2004
- Work in a collaborative setting with a team of six multilevel teachers in an urban school with students of varied abilities, ages 10 to 13 years.
- Responsibilities include initiating, planning, and implementing service learning projects; integrating reading and writing, grammar, phonics, and spelling into a holistic individualized curriculum; coordinating and teaching math lessons and activities; observing all subject areas and various teaching techniques; organizing homeroom and beginning-of-day activities for all students; planning, preparing and organizing materials for thematic units used by various age-groups.
- Enhanced and increased the use of computer technology in the class; and introduced and facilitated student portfolio development using multimedia and web-authoring software.

PRACTICA EXPERIENCE

3rd grade, all subjects, East Boulder Elementary, Fall 2003
4th–6th grade, community service project-environment and pollution, Grant School, 2002
Multiage, multimedia (computer basics, digital audio and video) Grant School, Fall 2002
Unit One, at-risk primary unit using integrated approach, Denver Public Schools, Spring 2002

PROFESSIONAL DEVELOPMENT SEMINARS AND ADVANCED COURSE WORK

Manual Communication   Linguistics   Classroom Management
Brain-based Learning   Exceptional Learner   Computer Programming

SERVICE

Volunteer Web master and computer skills instructor, Denver Senior Center, 2004 – present
Chairperson, Aviation for All Ages, Colorado Chapter, 2003 – present
Volunteer Air Rescue Squad (licensed pilot), Rockies Rescue Unit, 2001 – present

Electronic teaching portfolio at: www.jjefferson.du.education.edu

References available upon request.

THOMAS J. ANDREWS

3 University Avenue   Any City, State 21345
(101) 555-0009   cell: (909) 333-0003   tjandrews@kent.edu

TEACHING INTERESTS
Primary Grades (K-3)
Reading Recovery Experience

COACHING INTERESTS
Soccer - all levels
Assist in basketball, track
Coaching authorization - State of Ohio

EDUCATION
Kent State University, Kent, Ohio
Major: Elementary Education

B.A. Degree, May 2004
Minor: Anthropology

HONORS
Dean's List
Distinguished Senior Award

Tuition Scholars Award
Graduated with high distinction

FIELD EXPERIENCES
First-Grade Reading Recovery Program, Kent Public Schools, January 2003
Transitional First Grade, Pierce School, Kent, Spring 2004
Early Childhood Training Program, Department of Defense Dependents Schools,
*   Munich, Germany, Summer 2003*

Responsibilities during the above teaching positions included:
- Planning developmentally appropriate activities following weekly themes and organizing materials for thematic units in various areas
- Using systematic lesson planning emphasizing long- and short-term goals and assessment
- Implementating positive classroom management strategies
- Motivating students through an active learning environment
- Using basal and literature-based reading programs
- Communicating with parents through a weekly newsletter

PRACTICA
Kindergarten-intergenerational service learning project, Kent, Fall 2003
Reading Recovery Program, Hope Elementary, Kent, Summer 2003
Third-grade skills development (reading and writing), Kent Academy, Fall 2002

RELATED ACTIVITIES
Ohio Association for the Education of Young Children
Child Abuse Identification Training; CPR Certification
Pediatrics Volunteer, General Hospital, Kent, Ohio

ATHLETIC EXPERIENCE
All-Conference Soccer Selection
Coach, Kent Summer Soccer Camps

MVP Soccer Award
Soccer Coach, Kent Soccer Club

Credentials at Career Planning and Placement, Any City, State 21345   (101) 555-0008

TALYA MORGAN

3 University Avenue Any City, State 21345 (101) 555-0009
t-morgan@ug.edu

SKILLS
- Emphasis in early reading and language skills
- Experience in direct and indirect instruction for emergent and developing readers
- Training in cooperative learning, writing, storytelling, brain growth, and problem solving

EDUCATION

University of Georgia, Athens, Georgia, B.S. Degree – May, 2004
Majors in Elementary Education and Reading *Honors Commendation*

COURSE HIGHLIGHTS

Literature for Children   Early Literacy Development
Language and Society   Language Processing
Manual Communication   Cognitive Development

READING INTERNSHIP

Reading Clinic, Multiage Class, Lincoln Elementary, Athens, Spring 2004
Responsibilities:
- Developed, administered, and scored an Individualized Reading Inventory and Standardized Reading Inventory
- Made individual instructional assessments under guidance of mentor
- Assisted developing readers by using guided reading instruction including conferences and journaling activities
- Used reader's workshop strategies for developing readers using trade books and individual conferences
- Designed and maintained progress charts and conducted case studies
- Communicated with parents on a regular basis
- Attended Child Study team meetings and staffing meetings for learning disabled students

STUDENT TEACHING

4th and 5th grades, Salmon Elementary, Athens Public Schools, Fall 2003
Responsibilities:
- Collaborated with teaching teams in social studies, language arts, and math
- Organized and created learning centers stressing technology applications
- Assisted students in developing Hyperstudio presentations and taught digital camera and video for student computer demonstrations
- Provided one-on-one tutorial assistance in math

RELATED ACTIVITIES

Private tutor, reading, and math, Athens Summer Academy, 2004
Hospital Volunteer Pediatrics Unit, University Hospitals, 2003
Member, Athens Area Reading Council, 2003 – present

Credentials at Educational Career Office, Any City, State 21345 101.555.0008
View teaching portfolio at: www.talyamorgan@education.georgia.edu

MIMI ROCK-HARRIS

3 University Avenue   Any City, State 21345   (101) 555-0009   mrock-harris@pacific.edu

OBJECTIVE	Elementary General Music (K-6)
SPECIALIZED SKILLS	Training in Orff-Schulwerk and Kodaly methods Music technology, synthesizer, and audio technology Composer and creative producer
INTERNSHIP EXPERIENCE	Elementary General Music and Elementary Instrumental and Strings Tacoma Public Schools, Tacoma, Washington, September 2003 – May 2004 • Taught K-6 students in general and instrumental music classes • Used numerous strategies to motivate students to learn about and appreciate music from various cultural and ethnic backgrounds • Incorporated the use of keyboards, piano, and guitar into the classroom • Used Orff-Schulwerk and Kodaly teaching techniques with all ages • Served as a guest intern on school district committees, including Curriculum Development and Computer Applications for K-6
EDUCATION	Pacific Lutheran University, Bachelor of Music Degree - August 2004 Major: Music Education Emphasis: Trumpet Semester exchange program in Beijing, China, 2001
UNIVERSITY LEADERSHIP & ACTIVITIES	Elected President, Student Association-Music Educators Council, 2004 Teaching Assistant, Music Education, Seattle Pacific University, 2003 Received Student Educator-of-the Year Award, Bay Association, 2002 Wrote and directed two musicals for youth, 2001 Published: "Electronics in the Elementary Classroom," *Music Educator's Journal,* Vol. 12, pp. 28–32, 2001 Performer, Seattle Brass Choir (performed in Austria, Italy, and U.S. cities)
AFFILIATIONS	Music Educators National Conference; Northwest Music Educators Music Educators Association; National Education Association
HONORS	Outstanding Performer Award, Pacific Lutheran University Ken March Award for Talented Music Major, Pacific Lutheran University First Chair, Pacific Lutheran University Concert Band Composition Award and Dean's Recognition Award
RELATED EXPERIENCE	Instructor, Summer School at Pacific Music Institute, Seattle, 2004 – present Supervisor, Chamber Music at Snowmass, Colorado, Summer 2003 Dorm Assistant, Killington Music Festival, Rutland, Vermont, Summer 2002

Credentials at Career Development Office, Any City, State 21345 (101) 555-0008
View teaching portfolio at: www.mimi-rock-harris.education.pacific.edu

BROCK RAMONO

3 University Avenue   Any City, State 21345   (101) 555-0008   brock-ramono@stjohns.edu

TEACHING INTERESTS
Physical Education – elementary level
– Ability to adapt curriculum to students' interests, capabilities, and learning styles
– Training reflects sound curriculum and instructional techniques
– Knowledge of child development and learning strategies

Coaching – junior high sports
– Ability to teach basic team fundamentals to students of all abilities
– Coaching philosophy for this age-group includes learning group cooperation, goal setting, and lifetime fitness
– Interest in coaching volleyball, basketball, and track

EDUCATION
B.S. Degree, May 2004, St. John's University, Jamaica, New York
Major: Physical Education and Leisure Studies   Minor: Psychology

FIELD EXPERIENCES
Student Teaching: K-5 Physical Education, Jamaica County Schools, Spring 2003
Practicum: Island Primary Learning Center, Fall 2001; Mays Middle School, Fall 2002
– Worked in diverse settings as a collaborative team member
– Planned and taught lessons that were appropriate for the growth and development of primary-school and intermediate-aged children
– Created various units for different ages, including K-6 parachute unit, early childhood manipulatives unit, K-2 rhythms unit, and a middle school track and field unit; see lesson plans at: www.bramono.stjohn.education.htm
– Stressed cooperative learning, fitness, and lifelong leisure activities in unit plans
– Communicated curriculum and student's progress to parents on a regular basis

SERVICE AND LEADERSHIP
Volunteer coach, elementary track and field clinics, Jamaica YMCA, 2003
Cochair, Special Olympics Festival, New York Alliance, Inc., 2003 – present
Member, Intercollegiate Sports Council, St. John's University, 2003 – present
Letter winner, St. John's University Track and Field team, 2000 – 2003

Credentials at Career Development Office, Any City, State 21345 (101) 555-0008

CURT CROCKETT

3 University Avenue   Any City, State 21345   (101) 555-1111   curt-crockett@nmontana.edu

ACADEMIC INTERESTS AND TRAINING

Teaching Interests
Reading Recovery Specialist

Degrees
M.A., Reading, Northern Montana College, Havre, Montana, June 2004
  Thesis: "Self-esteem and reading ability in first-grade students"
  Adviser: Dr. Will B. Proff, Chair, Elementary Education
B.A., Elementary Education (developmental reading emphasis), May 2000

GRADUATE COURSES OF INTEREST

Building Foundations for Reading
Developmental Reading Skills
Seminar: Research and Current Issues

Diagnostic and Prescriptive Approaches
Advanced Reading Clinic Techniques
Brain Growth and Language Ability

CLASSROOM EXPERIENCE

Graduate Internship: Reading Recovery and Reading, Butte School, Helena, Montana, Fall 2003
– Under the supervision of a master reading clinician, used the Reading Recovery Model for individual students in the morning and taught in a reading resource room each afternoon
– Used five basic instructional activities in the reading resource room:
  (1) rereading a familiar book
  (2) reading a new book
  (3) mini-lessons
  (4) writing and editing
  (5) introducing a new book
– Carefully assessed students' abilities, evaluated progress, and communicated regularly with parents and classroom teachers.

Reading Practicum: English as a Second Language Classroom, Rocky Boy School, Box Elder, Montana, Spring 2003
– Taught reading to eleven-year-old students (one from Nigeria, the other from Argentina)
– Used various methods to reach students who were reading at first-grade level
– Organized basal, word attack, and language experience units
– Emphasized four goals during reading instruction:
  (1) comprehension
  (2) fluency
  (3) word identification
  (4) sight vocabulary

AFFILIATIONS, HONORS, AND ACTIVITIES

International Reading Association; Montana Reading Association; Arrow Area Reading Council Dean's Achievement Award; Reed A. Lott Scholarship, 2003; Pi Lambda Theta Member

References: Career Center, Any City, State 21345 (101) 555-0008
Teaching Portfolio: www.curtcrockett.education.umontana.htm

MARIA LOPEZ-BROWN

3 University Avenue, Any City, State 21345   (101) 555-0009

OBJECTIVE

Bilingual Early Childhood Special Education

SKILLS

- Work effectively with Spanish-speaking children and parents
- Develop Individual Education Plans (IEP), goals, and program objectives
- Design learning activities corresponding to IEP goals
- Implement effective behavior-management strategies for each student

DEGREE

B.A. Degree, Florida Atlantic University, Boca Raton, Florida, July 2004
Major: Special Education   Minor: Early Childhood

Diploma, American School of Torréon, Mexico, June 2000

INTERNSHIPS

Early Childhood Special Education, East School, Middleburg, Florida, Fall 2003
Taught eight students in a rural cooperative program. Duties included:
- Planning and implementing learning activities for students with varied abilities
- Creating learning activities that corresponded to IEP goals
- Organizing home instruction/incorporating skills across all developmental domains
- Developing with parents and staff appropriate behavior-management strategies
- Communicating with children and parents in Spanish

Early Childhood Practicum, HACAP, Boca Raton, Summer 2003
- Taught prekindergarten students in a private setting
- Developed units in drama, art activities, and beginning reading
- Assisted with preschool screenings in conjunction with area professionals
- Planned developmentally appropriate activities for various learning centers

Preschool Special Education Practicum, Wake Schools, Boca Raton, Spring 2003
- Taught four students ages two to four years in a county program
- Worked with students in all skill areas and observed mentor teacher
- Assessed students' strengths and implemented a program for each child

RELATED EMPLOYMENT

Early Childhood Teacher, Centro para Niños, Torréon. Mexico, 1999 – 2001
- Taught in a state-operated child-care center where Spanish was the primary language
- Worked closely with parents to provide appropriate health care and follow-up

References available upon request

KIM LU
3 University Avenue, Any City, State 21345
019.555.0009 (cell)   kim-lu@uoregon.edu

EDUCATION

B.S. - Special Education - Elementary Hearing Impaired
University of Oregon, Eugene   August 2000 – May 2004

Deaf Interpreter Training
Gallaudet University, Washington, D.C. summers 2000 – present

INTERNSHIPS

Student Teaching
Woodburn School, Eugene, Oregon, January – May 2003
- Planned and presented lessons in reading, language arts, and mathematics to students ranging from ages 7 to 10
- Worked with ungraded curriculum that emphasized total communication through an aural-oral approach
- With cooperating teacher and other team members, participated in parent conferences and home visits
- Observed and assisted with new student entrance and placement tests; collaborated with classroom teachers and support staff

Practicum Experience
Graham Bell School, September – December 2002
- Assisted with skills development in reading and mathematics
- Provided individualized instruction in manual communication and finger spelling
- Assisted in parent-infant program for children to age 3

ACTIVITIES

Counselor, Camp for the Deaf, Nanjemoy, Maryland, summers 2000 – present
- Supervise six campers, including deaf boys and their hearing brothers
- Teach archery, soccer, and volleyball skills; assist with other activities, including biking and basketball

Interpreter, Pattersons General Hospital, Eugene, 2001 – 2003
- Served as a volunteer interpreter for hearing-impaired patients or relatives to facilitate communication with hospital staff
- Interpreting assignments were arranged through the Department of Communication and Education, University of Oregon

MEMBERSHIPS

Oregon Association for the Deaf
Student Member, Oregon Education Association
Convention of American Instructors of the Deaf
Phi Kappa Alpha Fraternity

CREDENTIALS

Career Services Center, Any City, State 21345   101.555.0008
Portfolio available upon request

NELLIE LINDAHL

3 University Avenue • Any City, State 21345 • (101) 555-1111 • nellie-lindahl@livnet.edu

TEACHING INTERESTS AND SKILLS

- Skilled at teaching severely behaviorally disabled students in a multidisciplinary team approach
- Trained in behavior management, including aversive therapy and alternative discipline plans
- Experienced in support plans addressing consequences and proactive intervention strategies
- Adept at communicating student's needs to classroom teachers and parents

ACADEMIC BACKGROUND:

Long Island University-Brooklyn Campus, New York
> Bachelor of Science Degree, Special Education, May 2004
> Licensure: K-6 Special Education, Mild and Moderate Disabilities, State of New York

Universidad Granada, Granada, Spain
> Spanish Language and Literature, 2002

TEACHING INTERNSHIP EXPERIENCE:

Mental Disabilities, Primary Unit, Wright School, Brooklyn Borough District 18, Fall 2003

> Taught twelve students, ages six to eight, with varied mental disabilities. Worked with students in all skill areas; main emphasis was on concept development, language, and motor and self-help skills. Organized students in instructional groups; worked effectively with the child study team. Attended weekly staff meetings, participated in parent conferences, and initiated special parent newsletter.

PRACTICA EXPERIENCE:

Autism: University Hospital School, Brooklyn, 2003
> Worked one-on-one with a twelve-year-old autistic child.

Limited English Skills: Queens Elementary Summer School Program, Queens, 2003
> Taught fifth-grade students with limited English skills.

Severely and Profoundly Disabled: Fifth Street Developmental Center, Brooklyn, 2002
> Assisted severely disabled students with communication skills.

COLLEGE DISTINCTIONS AND MEMBERSHIPS:

President-elect, International Student Club   A.Z. Zolinsky Memorial Award Scholarship
Student Advisory Committee   Member, Council for Exceptional Children

VOLUNTEER AND RELATED WORK EXPERIENCE:

Behavior Disorders Teacher Associate, Brooklyn Opportunity School, Summer, 2003
Spanish Interpreter, St. Pius Hospital Emergency Department, 2002 – present (weekends)
Volunteer, Special Olympics Track Festival, Staten Island, 2000 – 2002

REFERENCES AND PORTFOLIO

Placement and Teacher Certification, Any City, State 21345
(101) 555-0008   FAX: (101) 555-1118

VERA GOODE

3 University Avenue, Any City, State 21345 (101) 555-0009
vera-goode@satuniv.edu

TEACHING SKILLS
Art Teacher – Middle School
- Special expertise in painting, sculpture, and multimedia
- Experience in designing integrated lessons in collaborative settings
- Technology skills in graphic design and various software applications

EDUCATION
B.F.A. Seattle University, May 2004
- International Study in Milan and Florence, Italy, 2002
- Kansas City Art Institute, 2001 – 2002

TEACHING INTERNSHIP
Art, Pacific Coast Middle School, Seattle, Spring 2004
- Teaching responsibilities included working with students in all classrooms, 5th – 8th grades
- Integrated lessons to reflect everyday activities and to include topics in science and social studies; lessons included bookmaking, painting, drawing, printmaking, weaving, metalworking and multimedia
- Created projects for all learners from inclusion students to non-English speakers
- Helped students display artwork in storefronts, local office buildings, and the Bay Museum

FIELD EXPERIENCE
Middle School and K-3 Art, Seattle Public Schools, Fall 2003
- Prepared lessons in ceramics, drawing, painting, calligraphy, puppet making, mixed media, and special research projects; organized several art shows and contests
- Guided an outdoor education art workshop for a team retreat
- Joined in child study teams and was available for after-school help on a daily basis

RECOGNITION
Academic
- Scholastic Art Award, Gold Key and Blue Ribbon
- Frank Jesper Scholarship

Art
- Group Show: Missouri Arts Show, Kansas City Art Center, 2003
- Juried Show: 40th Annual Seattle Artist's Show, Seattle, 2002
- Invitational Exhibition: Pacific Coast Invitational, Vancouver, 2001

PROFESSIONAL MATERIALS
Portfolio
- Web-based portfolio available for review or on-line at www.veragoode.education.htm
Recommendations
- Letters of reference at Education Placement Office, Any City, State 21345 (101) 555-0008

HATTIE SORENSEN–JASPER

3 University Avenue   Any City, State 12345   (101) 555-0009   hattie-s-jasper@umn.edu

TEACHING INTERESTS	Block Team Member Interdisciplinary	Mathematics Physical Education	Science Reading

RELATED INTERESTS
Coaching Softball, Swimming, and Basketball
Sponsoring student clubs and working with community groups
Working with technology issues and related computer-based projects

EDUCATION
University of Minnesota-Minneapolis
M.A. Degree, Curriculum and Instruction, May 2003
Concentration: Middle School Instruction
Emphasis: Mathematics, Reading, Science
B.S. Degree, *with honors,* Exercise Science, May 2000

Minnesota Teaching License, Elementary K – 6; Middle School 6 – 8
Minnesota Coaching Certificate, all sports

HONORS
Invited Member, Honors Program   Dean's List, 6 semesters
Twin Cities Women's Club Scholarship   Governor's Youth Award, 1998

INTERNSHIP EXPERIENCES
Resource Specialist, Special Semester Intern, St. Paul Schools, Spring 2002
Middle School Interdisciplinary Unit Intern, Central Magnet School, Fall 2001

Responsibilities of above internship experiences include:
– Planning educational objectives and lesson plans for interdisciplinary units
  for middle school students with a wide range of ability levels, including
  non-English speakers, special needs, and academically accelerated students
– Using various strategies, including cooperative learning, technology
  integration with emphasis on goal setting, and student responsibility
– Implementing positive and proactive classroom-management strategies
– Working in a team setting, attending in-service workshops and grade-level
  meetings
– Conducting parent-teacher conferences and student-led parent conferences

FIELD EXPERIENCE
Science Education, middle school   Math, grade 7
Physical Education, all ages   Language Arts, ages 9 – 13
General Education, ages 8 – 12   Reading, grades 7 and 8

ATHLETIC EXPERIENCE
Coach, St. Paul Youth Softball, Summers, 2000 – 2002
Head Student Athletic Trainer, Softball, University of Minnesota, 1999 – 2000
Summer Umpire, North Havenship Little League, 1999
Competitive Swimmer, 15 years

REFERENCES
References available upon request.
Portfolio at: www.umn.edu/hattie-portfolio.htm

LEE DeSILVA

• 3 University Avenue • Any City, State 21345 • (101) 555-0008 • lee-desilva@pennst.edu

OBJECTIVE AND STRENGTHS
Teacher: **Middle School Language Arts**

Strengths: **Apply an integrative approach to lesson design**
Emphasize multiculturalism in the classroom
Create authentic learning experiences
Strong background in the writing process, including grammar
    and usage
Emphasize technology integration
Experienced in collaborating with teaching teams, administration,
    parents, and guardians
Speak Spanish fluently

ACADEMIC BACKGROUND
University of Illinois – Champaign-Urbana   **August 2002 – May 2004**
- **M.A. Degree, English Education, May 2004**
  Thesis: "Assessment of Skills Development in Portfolios of Student Writing"
  Adviser: Dr. Willa Pruvitt, Department Chair
- **B.A. Degree, English, May 2000**   **Emphases: Spanish and Latin**
  American Studies
  Order of Omega National Greek Honor Society
  Honors Program and Dean's List

CLASSROOM EXPERIENCE
Student Teaching Internship - Language Arts, Acer Middle School, Urbana, Fall 2003
- Taught multiethnic students at all learning levels
- Initiated the development of writing portfolios; held regular conferences with students
- Participated in middle school team approach to teaching; prepared interdisciplinary lessons
- Incorporated cooperative-learning activities into the curriculum; provided peer tutoring
  services for students needing additional help

English 9 Practicum Experience, Lake Senior High School, Champaign, Spring 2003
- Taught thematic units on survival, disibilities, and fantasy; incorporated poetry, prose
  and drama; integrated reading and writing activities within the established curriculum
- Established daily journal writing in class

VOLUNTEER SERVICE
Instructor, English as a Second Language, Romania, July 2000 – August 2002
- Taught English conversation to grammar school students ages 8–13
- Created and developed curriculum and teaching materials
- Program sponsored by Education for Democracy/U.S.A., Inc.

INTERNATIONAL STUDY
Herencia Espanola, Madrid University, Madrid, Spain, Summer 2000
- Participated in 60 hours of Spanish language and culture classes and a week of travel in
  Spain with students from more than 30 countries

References and portfolio provided upon request.

SHERIFF TEWIZ

3 University Avenue, Any City, State 12345
(101) 555-0009   sheriff-tewiz@virginia.edu

DEGREES
University of Virginia, Charlottesville, Virginia
M.A. Education, Emphasis: Curriculum and Instruction for Middle School, June 2004
B.A. Elementary Education, Emphasis: Language Arts and Social Studies, May 1997

OBJECTIVE
Teacher: Middle School
Expertise: Language Arts - writing skills   Social Studies - thinking skills

STUDENT TEACHING
Rosa Parks Middle School, Norfolk, Virginia, February – June 2004
- Devised projects for individual investigation and small-group collaboration suitable for students with a wide range of interests and achievement levels
- Team-taught in an integrated Language Arts/Social Studies program, grades 6 – 8
- Used a Writer's Workshop mode of instruction to help students develop their writing skills
- Prepared units on history and biographies of the colonial period
- Created interest centers to emphasize contributions of women to colonial social and cultural history
- Practiced effective classroom-management techniques to promote student achievement
- Assisted with supervision of pupils in out-of-classroom activities
- Participated in grade-level-curriculum and team meetings and and participated in conferences to discuss student progress and interpret school expectations

PRACTICUM EXPERIENCE
Creative Arts Magnet School, Norfolk, Virginia, September – October 2003
- Observed team of three teachers employing an integrated approach to language arts and social studies instruction with students of exceptional abilities and a wide range of interests; observed team planning and evaluation sessions
- Participated in language arts instruction; worked with individual students on building vocabulary and enhancing reading skills; volunteered to assist with magazine layout

TECHNOLOGY INTEGRATION
- Integrated multimedia into lessons; taught students Web-authoring skills; encouraged parents to visit the Web site to learn about student research projects, reading lists, and conferences (view at: www.creativemagnetclass.Norfolk.edu.htm)
- Worked with various technologies including: digital video and cameras, photo imaging, web-authoring software, and basic computer programming (view teaching portfolio at: www.sheriffportfolio.education.virgina.edu.htm)

RELATED PROFESSIONAL WORK
Assistant Manager, The Computer Store, Norfolk, Virginia, July 1997 – May 2002
- Assisted customers with computer questions; rebuilt hard drives and installed software updates; taught basic computer-operating classes; handled supervisory staff duties

References available upon request

HOLLY BIRCH

3 University Ave.   Any City, State 12345   (101) 555-0009
holly-birch@odu.edu

TEACHING OBJECTIVE
Middle School Reading Teacher

EDUCATION
Old Dominion University, Norfolk, Virginia
B.A. Degree, June 2003   Major: Reading

Université de Lyon, Lyon, France
Year Abroad Program, 2001   Emphases: Literature and Art

COURSE HIGHLIGHTS

Middle School Reading Diagnostic Techniques	Literature for Children
Research and Current Issues in Reading	Building Foundations for Reading
Reading Clinic	The Politics of Literacy
Second Language Classroom Learning	Reading in a Second Language

EXPERIENCE
Teaching Internship
Middle School Developmental Reading, Norfolk Public Schools, Spring 2003
Major areas of teaching and related activities included:
- Word identification
- Sight vocabulary
- Comprehension
- Fluency
- Integrating of reading and writing
- Self-selected reading

Practica
High School Reading (9th grade), Metro Alternative Center, Norfolk, Fall 2002
Intermediate-Grade Reading, Edison Elementary School, Norfolk, Spring 1998
Advanced Reading for Gifted Students (3rd grade), St. Luke's Academy, Fall 1998

Language Ability
Fluent in French; lived with a French family, 1998, 2001
Good reading ability in Spanish, moderate speaking skills

RELATED ACTIVITIES
International Reading Association, Member, 2002 – present
Pen Pal Partner, Norfolk Neighborhood Projects, 2002 – present
Reader for the Blind, Old Dominion Special Services, 2002
Volunteer reader for Norfolk Senior Citizen's Center, 2000 – 2001

CREDENTIALS
References at Educational Career Services, Any City, State 12345 (101) 555-0008
Teaching portfolio available upon request.

CAREY J. SAYLOR

• 3 University Avenue • Any City, State 21345 • 101.555.1111 • cell: 019.555.0009 • cjsaylor@uiowa.edu

COMPETENCIES

SCIENCE	*MATH*	*SPONSOR/COACH*
Biology	Algebra	Science Club
Earth Science	Geometry	Math Bee
Environmental Studies	General Math	Varsity Baseball

DEGREES

The University of Iowa, Iowa City, Teacher Certification Program, Science Education, June 2004
Lake Forest College, Lake Forest, Illinois, B.A. Biology and Mathematics, May 2002
  Graduated with highest distinction   Dean's List   Presidential Scholar, 2001

INTERNSHIP EXPERIENCES

Middle School Science, Pierce Middle School, Cedar Rapids, Iowa, Fall 2003
Ninth-Grade Science, Linn-Mar High School, Marion, Iowa, Spring 2004
  • Taught Biology I, Environmental Studies, and Global Issues
  • Provided students the opportunity to use creativity and higher-order thinking skills
  • Developed rubrics for student group evaluations and portfolio assessment
  • Designed labs for all learners and provided materials for accelerated students
  • Created a life-science module centered around activities and investigations
  • Used constructivist learning theory in designing lessons, labs, and activities

PRACTICUM EXPERIENCE

Math and Science, Lincoln Middle School, Chicago Public Schools, Chicago, Illinois, Fall 2002
  • Assisted with teaching responsibilities in exploratory science
  • Required students to apply mathematical reasoning to problems
  • Organized and led small-group activities in advanced sixth grade math
  • Taught integrated unit with English Department on rain forests and global impact
  • Involved in supervising computer lab for seventh-grade math students

AFFILIATIONS

Student Member, National Science Teachers Association; Iowa State Education Association
Cochair, Campus Recycling Committee; Lake Pollution Coalition Board Member

ATHLETIC AND RELATED EXPERIENCES

Scholarship Baseball Player, All Conference Pitcher, MVP, Most Inspirational, 2000 – 2002
Math Tutor - University Special Support Services, The University of Iowa, 2002 – present

---

Credentials: Career Center, Any City, State 21345 101.555.0008 www.careers.university.edu
Electronic portfolio: www.carey-saylor.education.uiowa.edu. View documentation of teaching
skills, goals, labs and lab revisions, lesson planning, and assessment strategies.

Gary Polaska

3 University Avenue
Any City, State 21345
(101) 555-0009   *cell*: (345) 368-9989
gary-polaska@mail.com

OBJECTIVE
Secondary agriculture education teacher and club sponsor of extracurricular activities and events

EDUCATION
B.S. Degree, Purdue University, West Lafayette, Indiana, May 2004
Major: Agriculture Education, Teaching Certificate, Grades 7 – 12, December 2004
   Scholarship, Future Farmers of America (FFA)   Dean's List, 5 semesters

A.A. Degree, Indiana Vocational Technical College - Lafayette
Major: Agricultural Technologies - 2002

STUDENT TEACHING
Agriculture Education, South Putnam High School, Greencastle, Indiana, Fall 2004
Responsibilities:
- Developed and taught units on soil analysis and farm management
- Team-taught 2-week ecology unit with biology teacher using lab experiments, soil-testing techniques, and analysis procedures
- Arranged for Department of Agriculture scientists to present information to students about policy development and enforcement
- Cosponsored the Future Farmers of America with planning and supervision of club activities and fundraisers
- Graded FFA Proficiency Applications; judged competitions at the regional FFA meeting

RELATED EMPLOYMENT
Field research assistant, King Hybrid Seed Co., Vincennes, Indiana, Summer 2004
Research assistant, College of Agriculture, Purdue University, Fall 2003
Responsibilities in above positions included:
- Testing and analyzing new soybean varieties for use in wet climates
- Working closely with faculty and research scientists in field and lab environments

MEMBERSHIPS
- Student Member, Indiana Vocational Agriculture Teachers Association
- Secretary, Purdue Chapter, 2003; Program Planning Committee, 2003, Delegate - State Conference, 2004
- National Vocational Agriculture Teachers Association
- 4-H Member, 10 years; Officer, 4 years

CREDENTIALS
Career Services, Any City, State 21345 (101) 555-0008   Portfolio available upon request.

CHAD FOSTER

3 University Avenue, Any City, State 21345   (101) 555-0009   chad-foster@unm.edu

TEACHING INTERESTS	Alternative High School Instructor Community Liaison
STRENGTHS	Academic Strengths in English, History, Psychology, Computer Skills Student-Centered Approach with Emphasis on Goal Setting Strong Collaborative Skills
INTERNSHIP EXPERIENCE	Albuquerque Alternative Center, Fall 2003 – Worked in a diverse urban school alternative setting that fostered enthusiasm for learning by encouraging student participation – Involved students in goal setting and course and career planning – Used innovative methods and materials to produce effective learning experiences that built student pride and increased self-worth – Codeveloped, with mentor teachers, new course syllabi in Fine Arts – Encouraged students to take responsibility for their learning
PRACTICA	At-Risk Liaison, Spring Middle School, Taos, New Mexico, Fall 2002 – Counseled and worked closely with students who lacked basic skills, had extensive absences, or were failing due to home situations, jobs, or poor study habits. – Communicated with parents/guardians, parole officers, and social agencies regularly – Maintained careful records; documented activities and academic progress
DEGREES	M.A. English Education and Alternative Education, May 2003 University of New Mexico - Albuquerque B.A. Majors in Psychology and English, Minor in History, July 2001 Stanford University, Stanford, California
PART-TIME WORK	Web page developer, Mountain Electronics, 2002 – present Piano and bass teacher, private instruction, 2000 – present Acoustical and electric bass performer and sound manager, Mountain Jazz, 2002 – present

References available at Teacher Career Center, Any City, State 21345 (101) 555-0008

VERONICA ROYAL

3 University Avenue
Any City, State 21345
101.555.0008   v-royal@wustl.edu

OBJECTIVE

Art teacher, grades 7–12
- Specialized strengths in multimedia, photography, bookmaking, printmaking, and drawing
- Experience in collaborative planning, technology integration, and multicultural settings

ACADEMIC TRAINING

Bachelor of Fine Arts; Studio Emphasis: Printmaking   Washington University, St. Louis, May 2004
Honors: Phi Beta Kappa, Dean's List, Art Education Scholarship

TEACHING EXPERIENCE

Internship, St. Louis Public Schools, September 2003 – May 2004
High School Art, Lincoln High School, and Printmaking, Fine Arts Center, St. Louis
- Prepared educational objectives and lesson plans for painting, drawing, sculpture, and jewelry courses at Lincoln High School; assisted with teaching responsibilities in photography
- Organized student exhibits at the school and the city art museum
- Submitted student work for consideration in the Missouri Young Artist's Review
- Offered before-school art sessions for enrichment and started a photography club
- Attended faculty meetings, participated in school-improvement team meetings, volunteered at school functions, and worked with students participating in service-learning activities

Internship, Fine Arts Center, St. Louis, Spring 2004
- Taught art at three different centers.
- Created units in bookmaking, metals, multimedia, pottery, fabric design, and multicultural units on Egypt and Mexico
- Prepared exhibits for community viewing; organized educational sessions for service groups
- Involved in interdisciplinary planning with Center staff, area educators, and artists

EXHIBITS

Hands Gallery Photography Exhibition, Kansas City, June – August, 2004
Mississippi Annual Exhibition, Quad Cities Art Center, Davenport, Iowa, 2003

RELATED ART EXPERIENCE

Saturday Morning Art Workshop, Art Department, Washington University, Fall 2003
Art Tutor Volunteer, Eastside Youth Project, St. Louis, 2001 – 2003
Artist in Residence, North High School, East St. Louis Public Schools, 2002

PROFESSIONAL ORGANIZATIONS

National Art Education Association, Women's Caucus for Art, National Education Association

References and multimedia portfolio available upon request

B. J. LONG - SMITH

• 3 University Ave. • Any City, State 21345 • 101.555.1111 • bjl-smith@nau.edu

TEACHING INTERESTS AND SKILLS

Business Education – Secondary level
- Teaching strengths in Information Processing, Computer Technology, Keyboarding, Accounting, Business Law, Personal Finance, General Business, and Entrepreneurship
- Collaborative and multidisciplinary team approach
- Experience in business management with strong community connections

ACADEMIC BACKGROUND

Northern Arizona University, Flagstaff, Arizona
    Bachelor of Science Degree, Business Education, May 2004
    Licensure: 7–12 Business Education, State of Arizona
Universidad Granada, Granada, Spain
    Spanish Language and Literature, 2003
Mesa Community College, Mesa, Arizona
    Associate of Arts Degree, Accounting, December 1999

TEACHING INTERNSHIP EXPERIENCE

Business Education Department, South High School, Phoenix Public Schools, Fall 2003
- Taught beginning and advanced courses in keyboarding and accounting
- Taught students in advanced computer technology HTML and other web-development software packages
- Developed a three week head teaching unit for the upperclass Personal Finance course using various instructional strategies
- Worked closely with mentor teacher and with community representatives in placing and supervising high school students in the school-to-work program
- Attended weekly staff meetings, participated in open house, and observed parent/guardian conferences

PROFESSIONAL BUSINESS EXPERIENCE

Account Assistant, Borwne, Smith and Jackson, Ltd., Phoenix, Arizona, January 1999 – August 2002
    Responsibilities included research assignments for new tax laws regarding off-shore corporations. Duties required careful attention to detail, computer management, and teamwork. Traveled to numerous international sites to gather information and record details. Used Spanish-speaking translation skills for the accounting team.

CURRENT MEMBERSHIPS AND ACTIVITIES

President, Student Business Educators' Association	Zolins Memorial Award Scholarship
Student Advisory Committee, Northern Arizona University	Member, Phoenix Business Club
Spanish Interpreter, St. Pius Hospital Emergency Department	Volunteer, Special Olympics Track Festival

REFERENCES AND PORTFOLIO

Placement and Teacher Certification, Any City, State 21345   101.555.0008   FAX: 101.555.1118

SASHA LAWRENCE

3 University Avenue, Any City, State 21345
101.555.0009 sasha@haverford.edu

OBJECTIVE

Advanced-Placement English Instructor

EDUCATION

Haverford College, Haverford, Pennsylvania
Bachelor of Arts Degree, May 2004   Major: English   Minor: Spanish
Teacher Certification Program, Secondary English
Honors and Awards
A.J. Fine Scholarship in English Education
Brooke Memorial Scholarship, Department of English
Honors Program, President's List, Dean's List

HIGH-SCHOOL INTERNSHIP

Jones Academy, Philadelphia Public Schools, Spring 2003
- Taught Sophomore English in a school implementing a dual language pilot program at the lower grades, Advanced-Placement English to juniors, and Publications to all levels
- Worked cooperatively with students who were culturally and linguistically diverse using various instructional strategies to encourage all students to achieve their potential
- Prepared a comprehensive unit on the research paper for advanced-placement students
- Created units for Advanced-Placement English on Tennessee Williams's plays, as well as the novels *In Our Time*, *The Sound and the Fury*, *Ragtime*, *The Great Gatsby*, and *The Chosen*
- Incorporated use of recursive writing process, literature circles, alternate assessments, and guest speakers into the curriculum in a block scheduling system
- Cofacilitated Publications class and instructing students in elements of graphic design and the use of PageMaker software and digital cameras for student publications

MIDDLE-SCHOOL INTERNSHIP

Haverford Middle School and Stone City Junior High, Fall 2002 and Spring 2003
- Assisted with teaching responsibilities in sixth- and eighth-grade language arts classrooms
- Involved in supervising class drama production and video projects, responded to student journals, conducted student writing conferences and peer review workshops, read to students, and assisted special needs students in developing their reading, writing, and listening skills
- Initiated several organizational systems for managing cooperating teacher's paper load

EMPLOYMENT

University of Pennsylvania Upward Bound Project
- Teaching Assistant for Language Arts, Geometry, and Algebra classes, Summer 2003
- Women's Dormitory Night Monitor, Summer 2002
Haverford Parking Office
- Student Parking Clerk, August 2001 – January 2002

AFFILIATIONS

National Council of Teachers of English, Haverford College Acting Guild, Stone Players of Maine

PORTFOLIO AND CREDENTIALS

Writing portfolio available upon request.
References available at Career Office, Any City, State 21345   101.555.0008   www.haverford.careers.edu

MIA KIOTA

3 University Ave., Any City, State 21345   101.555.0009   mia-kiota@bc.edu

OBJECTIVE   Teacher - English as a Second Language

DEGREES   Advanced Studies - Linguistics, Boston College, June 2003
                     B.A. German and Japanese, Smith College, May 2001

LANGUAGE   *Second Language Education and Linguistic Course Work*
BACKGROUND   • Second Language Classroom Learning
                     • Fundamentals of Second Language Assessment
                     • Syntactic and Phonological Theory; Linguistic Structures
                     • Psycholinguistics and Anthropological Linguistics

                     German and Japanese
                     • Extensive course work in German and Japanese language and culture
                     • Participated in advanced language program in Austria, 2003
                     • AFS Student to Karlstadt, Germany, junior year
                     • Worked extensively with a Japanese tutor to enhance speaking skills
                     • Traveled to Japan, Summer 2002

                     Travel and Study Abroad
                     • Extensive travel in Europe and Japan
                     • Studied at the Regents Summer Program in Tokyo, 2000
                     • Intensive language study in St. Radegund
                     • Advanced language study, University of Vienna Hochschulekurs

                     Other Language Experience
                     • Resided for three years in the Smith College Foreign Language Residence Hall
                     • Involved in various intercultural exchanges with foreign students from Japan, Germany, China, Nepal, Brazil, France, Syria, and other countries
                     • Participated in campus presentations and public intercultural activities
                     • Shared experiences and language study with other students who lived abroad or traveled extensively

TEACHING   *Student Teaching:* Central Senior High School, Wells Elementary, Fall 2003
EXPERIENCE   • English language assessment and instruction for children with limited or no English language skills from 15 different countries

                     Practicum: Bay Intermediate School, Boston, Summer 2002
                     • Assisted with instruction of two classes of introductory German, and two classes of 7th-grade German
                     • Worked with students individually and in small groups

                     Language Lab Attendant: Smith College, 1999 – 2001
                     • Assisted users with language lab technology, answered questions, provided students with resources to complete assignments
                     • Monitored lab equipment and installed new software

Credentials available: Career Planning and Placement Center, Any City, State 21345 101.555.0008

REED A. LOTT

3 University Avenue, Any City, State 21345   (101) 555-0009
reed-a-lott@olaf.edu

OBJECTIVE English Instructor

SKILLS
- Academic training in Literature (traditional and contemporary) and Writing (creative, poetry, memoir, fiction, and nonfiction)
- Focus on critical reading and continuing literacy beyond classroom
- Collaborate with teaching teams, administration, guardians/parents
- Infuse technology into the classroom via computer writing labs, specialized software, and Internet applications

DEGREE B.A., English Literature, May 2004, St. Olaf College, Northfield, MN
(Graduated with highest distinction)

INTERNSHIP English, Madison High School, St. Paul Public Schools, Fall 2003
Theater, Loon Acting Academy, Northern Lakes, Summer 2002

Responsibilities included preparation of objectives and lesson plans for three grade levels in a collaborative setting. Extensive instruction in writing strategies and techniques in all classes. Taught 10th grade American Literature and Language class and several theater courses. Worked closely with students in acting classes and performances. Supervised computer writing lab and initiated special study review.

SPEECH Volunteer Speech Assistant, Northfield High School, 2002 – 2003

Assisted with play productions and coached members of the speech team involved in interpretation events. Traveled to meets and supervised students.

Speech Practicum, Jones Junior High School, Spring 2002

Worked with three sections of students in an elective speech class. Led small-group discussions and worked with students individually.

RELATED ACTIVITIES Actor, Loon Players Repertory Company & Atlas Community Theater
Member and stagehand, Northern Lights Center for the Arts, 3 years
Cashier and stocker, College Book & Supply, 2 years
(Financed schooling through part-time employment and loans)

PROFESSIONAL AFFILIATIONS Minnesota Communication Association; Speech Council of St. Paul
National Council of Teachers of English; Atlas Teachers Acting Guild

References and portfolio available upon request.

J. B. CUSTER

3 University Avenue, Any City, State 21345   101.555.0009
j-custer@cudenver.edu

TEACHING SKILLS

History Teacher, grades 9 – 12
- Special expertise in world history, European history, government
- Interest in assisting in student government, model United Nations, debate
- Experience in designing integrated lessons in collaborative settings
- Technology skills in graphic design and various software applications

EDUCATION

B.A. *with distinction* University of Colorado – Denver, May 2003
- International Study in Milan and Florence, Italy, 2002

STUDENT INTERNSHIP

Secondary Social Studies, Denver Public Schools, Fall 2002
- Prepared educational objectives and lesson plans for three levels. Worked with individuals, small groups, and large groups using various teaching strategies. Internship consisted of full-day, full-semester experience. Worked extensively with the following classes:

  – *European History:* Taught ancient and medieval European history to 10th and 11th graders. Developed a 2-week unit on the topic of serfdom and the political implications of power; used assessment strategies including document-based writing exercises, quizzes, group projects, and final exams to determine needs of students. Concentrated on students' research and writing skills in preparation for the national examination.

  – *African and Latin America:* Used simulations, multimedia, guest speakers, and small group activities to familiarize students with issues and problems confronting lesser-developed countries. Topics included development, debt, environment, and international relations. Concentrated on verbal and critical-thinking skills.

  – *World History:* Developed several units on medieval history designed around the learning needs of remedial students. Incorporated multimedia hands-on projects, take-home and oral examinations, and individual projects based on a contract for completion. Was available for after-school help on a daily basis. Concentrated on verbal and critical thinking skills.

RELATED EXPERIENCES

High School Government Practicum, Stone School, Denver, 2002
Tutor, Community Adult Learning Center, Denver, 2001 – 2002
Big Brother/Big Sister Partner, Denver, 2000 – present

PORTFOLIO & REFERENCES

On-line portfolio available for review at: www.edu.cudenver.jbcuster.htm
Education Placement Office, Any City, State 12345   101.555.0008

KRISTI HARRIMAN

3 University Avenue, Any City, State 21345
(101) 555-0009   kristi-harriman@tamu.edu

TEACHING COMPETENCIES AND INTERESTS

Home Economics	**Health**	**Sponsor**
Life Skills	Substance Abuse	Medical Sciences Club
Interior Design	Disease Prevention	International Club
Career Education	Consumer Health	SADD

ACADEMIC TRAINING

B.S. Degree, Home Economics and Health, Texas A&M University, College Station, May 2004
Dean's List   Alice Howe Internship Scholarship   graduated *with distinction*

INTERNSHIPS

Life Skills and Home Economics, East High School, College Station Schools, Spring 2004
- Worked in a culturally diverse setting with students pursuing vocational career tracks.
- Enriched curriculum with primary resource speakers from community agencies.
- Worked closely with local businesses to establish job-shadowing experiences as well as long-term internships.
- Developed teaching units in the following classes:
  - Independent Living
  - Cooking
  - Personal Finances
  - Family Planning
  - Issues in Health

Health, Sauk Middle School and Grant Elementary, Houston Public Schools, Fall 2003
- Assisted with teaching responsibilities in health; developed a unit on personal health care and sex education grades 6 – 8; led small-group activities and organized follow-up sessions.
- Volunteered to supervise after-school study lab and to work with students individually.
- Created a multidisciplinary unit on drugs and their consequences for grades 4 – 6.
- Enriched curriculum by inviting medical professionals to talk to students about addiction and prevention strategies.

Credentials: Career Center, Any City, State 21345   (101) 555-0008   www.careers.edu
Electronic Portfolio: www.education.tamu.kharriman/ed.edu

IZZY HIGGINS

3 University Ave., Any City, State 21345
101-555-0009 (home) 101-555-1111 (cell)
izzy-higgins@hamline.edu

TEACHING INTERESTS	Journalism Teacher Student Publication Adviser

EDUCATIONAL INTERNSHIPS	Student Intern, Journalism Department, St. Paul Public Schools, Summer 2004
	Intern, Newspaper Writing, Egan Valley Schools, Spring 2003
	   – Responsibilities included teaching classes in Foundations of Journalistic Writing, Advertising and Mass Media
	   – Supervised Newsmagazine Lab and held workshops on journalistic writing, design, desktop publishing, editing, and pasteup
	   – Assisted students in campaign to increase advertising sales
	   – Structured lessons to meet the needs of each individual and met with students seeking additional assistance with course work or technology
	   – Formally assessed student performance for mid- and end-of-term grading
	   – Chaperoned trip to Minnesota High School Press Association conference

DEGREE	Bachelor of Arts Degree, School of Journalism and Mass Communication, August 2004
	Hamline University, St. Paul, Minnesota
	   Honors: Carl Hansen Writing Scholarship *Dean's List*
	      summa cum laude

TECHNOLOGY	Proficiency in QuarkXPress, PageMaker, PhotoShop, Dreamweaver, FrontPage, Excel Digital video and audio, and standard photographic equipment
PRESENTATIONS	"Teaching Students Their Rights as Young Editors," Preconference workshop presentation, Association for Education in Journalism and Mass Communication, New Orleans, August 2004 "Newspaper Labs in High Schools: Partnerships with Local Newspapers," address at State Conference for High School Journalism Teachers, Atlanta, May 2003 Panel Member, "Ethics in Reporting: Whose Ethics?" Investigative Reporters and Editors Conference, West Palm Beach, October 2002

WRITING EXPERIENCE	Staff Writer, *Hamline Times*, Hamline University, 2002 – present
	   Cover education and city hall news. Supervise students in the High School Reporting Internships Program sponsored by the *Hamline Times*.
	Minnesota Press Journalist, Minneapolis, June 2002 – January 2003
	   Generated story ideas, interviewed sources, and wrote news and feature stories for a regional magazine with a circulation of over 30,000. Used QuarkXPress in editing and layout.

PORTFOLIO	View examples of writing skills: magazine articles, newspaper stories, university courses View student artifacts: yearbook, newspaper at: www.izzy-higgins.journalism.hu.edu
REFERENCES	University Career Center, Any City, State 21345 101-555-0008

SUSIE Q. JOSEPHS

3 University Avenue   Any City, State 21345   101.555.1111   susie-josephs@stanford.edu

ACADEMIC INTERESTS AND TRAINING

Teaching Interests: French and German Instructor

Degrees: Stanford University
Master of Arts Degree, Foreign Language Education, June 2004
  Thesis: "Language comprehension in second-generation adolescents"
  Adviser: Dr. Will B. Proff, Chair, Foreign Language Education
Bachelor of Arts Degree, Major: French, Minor: German and History, May 2000

GRADUATE COURSES OF INTEREST

Restructuring Language Classes   Teaching K-12 Second Language Learners
Second Language Classroom Learning   Linguistic Diversity in the Classroom
Research and Current Issues   Brain Growth and Language Ability

CLASSROOM EXPERIENCE

Graduate Internship: French Immersion School, San Jose, California, Spring 2004
- Worked in a team setting and planned cooperatively with colleagues from all departments
- Taught one unit of math and two units of science, using various techniques, including cooperative learning and hands-on exploration of scientific and mathematical concepts
- Used various assessment techniques including pretesting and posttesting, journaling, rubrics, and oral and written presentations; carefully assessed students' abilities, evaluated progress, and communicated regularly with parents and classroom teachers
- Participated in two cultural celebrations, open houses, staff meetings, and in-service workshops

Practica: Palo Alto High School, Secondary German, Fall 2003
- Under supervision of a master teacher, planned, instructed, and assessed German I, II, IV
- Worked closely with individual students in grammar, basic writing, and pronunciation skills
- Developed supplementary teaching materials to use in the classroom and incorporated current events via the Internet whenever possible

ESL Fieldwork: Nymphenburger Gymnasium, Munich, Germany, Summer 2003
- Directed three sections of English as a Second Language to middle- and high-school-age students in a summer-school setting stressing conventional English-language uses
- Incorporated U.S. current events in the classroom and used games and activities to increase cultural understanding and compare the structure and use of the English and German languages

AFFILIATIONS AND HONORS

Member, American Association of Teachers of French; Member, California Council on the Teaching of Languages and Cultures; President's Achievement Award; Pi Lambda Theta, Phi Beta Kappa

References: Career Center, Any City, State 21345 101.555.0008
Teaching Portfolio: www.suzie-josephs.education.standford.htm

J. J. CHRISTOPHERSEN

3 University Avenue, Any City, State 21345   (101) 555-0009
jjchristophersen@purdue.edu

OBJECTIVE	Japanese Language and Culture, grades 6 – 12 English as a Second Language (ESL), all levels
DEGREES	B.A. Degree, May 2004, Purdue University, West Lafayette, IN Majors: Linguistics and Japanese with teacher licensure
INTERNSHIP	Japanese, grades 6 – 12, Bellton Academy, Chicago, Spring 2004 – Taught Japanese on four levels including an Honors Class – Assisted in the coordination of interdisciplinary projects with social studies classes and art classrooms – Integrated technology into daily teaching with specialized software – Developed alternative assessment methods, including portfolios
ESL EXPERIENCE	English Teacher, Osaka Schools, Osaka, Japan, 2001 – 2003 – Team-taught, with Japanese mentor, English in three high schools – Created daily lesson plans on grammar, spelling, and vocabulary – Developed numerous supplementary teaching materials to use in the classroom and to share with students for nightly review – Presented seminars and workshops to area teachers and participated in several cultural exchange programs
AFFILIATIONS	Indiana Second Language Educators Association of Teachers of Japanese
PART-TIME WORK	Interpreter, Wong Travel Agency, Chicago, summers 2003 – present Tutor, Japanese language, private students, 2002 – present Web page designer, Indiana Design Solutions, 2001 – 2002
REFERENCES	Available upon request. Visit my Web site at www.christophersen.portfolio.htm to view documentation of teaching skills, lesson planning, parent communication, bilingual abilities, and assessment strategies.

NATASHA BUTIN

3 University Avenue, Any City, State 21345
101.555.0009   natasha-butin@rice.edu

OBJECTIVE
Teacher: Russian Language (9 – 12)   Sponsor: International Club

EDUCATION
Rice University, Houston, Texas   B.S. Degree – May 2003   *with honors*
      Major: Russian Language
      Minor: Linguistics
      Teacher Licensure - Texas and Colorado

The Pushkin Institute, Moscow, Russia Exchange Program, July 2001 – May 2002

Colorado Summer Russian Seminar, Colorado Springs, Colorado, Summer 2000

INTERNSHIP
Russian Language, Valley High School, Denver Public Schools, Spring 2003

Responsibilities:
      Reviewed curriculum resources and created new materials and prepared lesson plans and objectives
         for levels I–IV
      Organized and created grammar explanations, games, and activities and effectively used cooperative-
         learning strategies in delivery of materials
      Stressed higher-order thinking skills by encouraging students to weigh information and consider other
         viewpoints from a cultural point of view
      Served as a sponsor of International Club and attended departmental meetings and support groups for
         international and exchange students

PRACTICUM EXPERIENCE
English as a Second Language, Boulder Middle School, Boulder, Summer 2002

Responsibilities:
      Assisted in all teaching responsibilities under the direction of mentor teacher
      Planned lessons for individual students, small groups, and whole class; adapted lessons for
         diverse student learning styles
      Used various management strategies and assessed instruction with daily reflections and
         journaling and regular conferences with cooperating teachers and university supervisors

CLASSROOM TECHNOLOGY
Integrated multimedia and Web-based authoring and management skills uploading all lesson plans,
    reflections, and assessments using a daily Web-based calendar in field experiences. Go to:
    www.natashaportfolio.rice.edu

ACTIVITIES
Member, American Association of Slavic and Eastern European Languages
Member, Dobro Slovo, Slavic Honor Society, President, Russian Circle, Rice University
Rice Marching and Concert Band (percussion specialist)

Credentials at Teacher Career Center, Any City, State 21345 101.555.0008

ANASTASIA PETIVOU

3 University Avenue   Any City, State 12345   (101) 555-0009   anastasia@ukans.edu

TEACHING COMPETENCIES

Spanish: Grammar, Latin American Culture, Spanish Culture, Literature, History
Journalism: News Reporting, Journalistic Writing, Photography, Broadcast Journalism

EXTRACURRICULAR INTERESTS

International Advisor	Student Government	Yearbook Sponsor
Swimming Instructor	Cheerleading Sponsor	Newspaper Advisor

EDUCATION

University of Kansas, Lawrence, Kansas
    Master's Degree, May 2003, Spanish with K-12 licensure
    Bachelor's Degree, May 2000, Double Majors: Journalism and Spanish

International Language Study, Mexico City and Barcelona, Spain, 2000 and 2002

FIELD EXPERIENCES

Spanish Intern, Roosevelt High School, Kansas City, Kansas, Fall 2002
Journalism Intern, North High School, Kansas City, Kansas, Fall 2002
  • Taught Spanish classes on levels I, II, III, and IV
  • Used effective classroom-management techniques
  • Provided tutorial services for students needing additional help
  • Incorporated special activities and guest speakers into curriculum
  • Evaluated student progress and held regular student conferences
  • Organized and led small-group activities focusing on ethics in journalism
  • Developed and taught a unit on magazine writing and editing
  • Supervised newspaper lab using desktop publishing technologies
  • Attended faculty workshop: "Preparing for Effective Online Instruction"

ACTIVITIES AND SERVICE

Member, American Council for the Teaching of Foreign Languages, 2003 – present
Staff writer, *Lawrence Daily News*, summers 2002, 2003
Volunteer cheerleading sponsor, City High School, 2002
Camp counselor - Camp Redwood, Mountain Top, Idaho, 2000, 2001

TECHNOLOGY KNOWLEDGE

Digital imaging	Software usage for rubrics, grades, schedules
Web management and design skills	Integrating multimedia into subjects

Credentials and portfolio at Career Planning and Placement, Any City, State 12345   (101) 555-0008

TED IRONSIDE

3 University Avenue, Any City, State 21345   cell: 101.555.0009
ted-ironside@sewanee.edu   www.ironside.education.edu

TEACHING COMPETENCIES

| Advanced Algebra and Calculus | Algebra and Geometry | Statistics |
| General Mathematics | Trigonometry | Computer Programming |

- Completed Principles of Technology training
- Knowledge of national math standards and essential academic learning
- Instructional skills include questioning strategies and concept development
- Use technology in advanced and basic classes to demonstrate concepts and to teach computer skills

EDUCATION

B.S. Degree – Mathematics, May 2002 – May 2004, University of the South, Sewanee, TN
- *Dean's List*   • *Presidential Citation*   • *Stephen Math Scholarship*
A.A. Degree – Mathematics, August 2001, Volunteer State Community College, Gallatin, TN

FIELD EXPERIENCE

Internship: High School Mathematics, Sewanee County Schools, January – May 2004
- Taught algebra, geometry, and calculus in a regional school using various teaching and motivational strategies to encourage students to reach their potential
- Identified areas of difficulty and prepared lessons to assist students
- Incorporated computer programs to increase problem-solving and reasoning abilities
- Used various preassessment and postassessment strategies, examinations, and rubrics
- Volunteer supervisor of Math Club and Computer Programming Club

Practicum: Middle School Mathematics, Pine Elementary, Martin Schools, May – July 2003
- Taught students of varied abilities in a grade 6/7 combination classroom
- Designed special activities to demonstrate math concepts
- Reinforced learning through computer-assisted instruction
- Attended meetings and school events and participated in parent-teacher conferences

RELATED ACTIVITIES

Tutor in basic computer applications, Sewanee and Nashville, 2003 – present
Dorm Clerk, Pikes Towers, University of the South, Sewanee, 2002 – 2004
Student Member, National Council of Teachers of Mathematics

References Provided Upon Request

LOTTE NOYES

3 University Avenue • Any City, State 21345
(319) 555-1111 • lotte-noyes@uhawaii.edu

TEACHING INTERESTS

K-12 Instrumental or General Music
- Concert, jazz, marching and pep bands, ensembles, private and large-group instruction
- Skills in piano, percussion, guitar, and all band instruments

ACADEMIC TRAINING

Bachelor of Music Degree, May 2004, University of Hawaii - Honolulu
Major: Music Education, K-12   Emphasis: Percussion
Honors: *with distinction*, Dean's List, Academic Music Performance Scholarship

STUDENT TEACHING AND PRACTICA EXPERIENCE

- High school and elementary instrumental music, Honolulu Schools, Fall 2003
- Middle school instrumental and elementary general music practica, Spring 2002
  Planned and prepared instructional plans emphasizing long- and short-term goals and assessment. Implemented positive management strategies and encouraged students from diverse backgrounds to participate. Effectively conducted full band and small ensembles. Instructed students on all band instruments during individual or group lessons.

RELATED ACTIVITIES

Private music instructor, guitar and piano, 2003 – present
All-State Music Camp Instructor, University of Hawaii, summers 2000 – 2001

PERFORMANCE ACCOMPLISHMENTS – University of Hawaii

Jazz Band and Jazz Ensembles
Symphonic Orchestra and Band (performances in Oregon, Minnesota, Ohio, New York)
Marching Band (performances at Rose Bowl Parade, Aloha Bowl, Kick-Off Classic)

OTHER WORK EXPERIENCE

Clerk, Pediatric Department, University Hospitals and Clinics, two years
University Computer Lab Assistant, Wilson and Danner Hall, three years

COMPUTER TECHNOLOGY

- Finale and Music Shop software, PhotoShop, multimedia skills (digital video and audio)
- Electronic Portfolio: Go to www.lnoyes.ed.uhawaii.htm to view music performance, documentation of teaching skills, lesson planning, and parent communication.

References available upon request.

JODY DENVER

3 University Avenue, Any City, State 21345   101.555.0009
www.jdenver.uaa.alaska.edu/portfolio
jdenver@uaa.alaska.edu

COMPETENCIES

VOCAL
Vocal Instruction
Concert and Swing Choirs
Choir (7th–12th)
Ensembles

SPECIAL INTERESTS
Contest Entries
All-State Participation
State and Regional Contests
Music Booster Club

ACADEMIC TRAINING

University of Alaska - Fairbanks, Teacher Certification Program
K - 12 Music, December 2003

Arizona State University - Tempe, Bachelor of Music Degree,
Voice Performance, May 2000
Honors: *Arizona State Music Scholarship; Dean's List, 7 semesters; graduated with distinction*

INTERNSHIP

H.S. Music, Yukon Flats High School, Beaver, Alaska, Fall 2003
Taught instrumental and vocal music appreciation classes
Used elements such as melody, harmony, rhythmic notation, form,
  and analysis
Provided tutorial services for students seeking advanced training
Incorporated cultural songs and special native Alaskan activities
Evaluated student progress by offering private lessons and small-group
  sessions
Performed local concerts and participated in regional contests

FIELD EXPERIENCE

Middle School Vocal Music, Yukon Middle School, Spring 2002
Assisted with teaching responsibilities in general music classes
Worked with small-group music ensembles
Reviewed music curriculum and related teaching materials

ACTIVITIES

University Concert Choir, Arizona State
Member, Arizona State Chamber Singers
Leading roles in two operas
Performed in numerous musicals

OTHER EXPERIENCE

All-State music instructor and camp supervisor - Arizona State
  All-State Summer Camp, 2000
Private music lessons - vocal and violin - Tempe and Fairbanks,
  summers 1998 – present

Credentials at Teacher Placement Center, Any City, State 21345   101.555.0008

NIKKI PAPPELLIS

3 University Avenue, Any City, State 21345
101.555.0009   npappellis@isu.edu

TEACHING AND COACHING INTERESTS
Physical Education Instructor, K – 12; Adaptive Physical Education Instructor, K – 8
Tennis Coach, High School

ACADEMIC PREPARATION
Degree: Iowa State University, Ames, Iowa, Bachelor of Science Degree – May 2004
              Major: Exercise Science with emphasis in Physical Education
              Minor: Special Education
Licensure: Iowa Professional Teaching License, Physical Education, grades K – 12
              Adaptive Physical Education Endorsement, grades K – 8
              State of Iowa Coaching Authorization

TEACHING INTERNSHIPS
Elementary Physical Education, Edwards Elementary School, Ames, Iowa, Fall 2003
High School Physical Education, Ames High School, Ames, Iowa, Fall 2003
Adaptive Physical Education, Nevada Elementary School, Nevada, Iowa, Summer 2003
   Responsibilities:
   • Taught students at all levels from kindergarten to high school seniors
   • Used various teaching techniques to allow for differing learning styles
   • Worked with adaptive physical education students and developed appropriate skill-level activities
   • Established an active learning environment through positive feedback
   • Assisted with the organization of the Heart Association's Jump Rope for Heart
   • Observed special education classes and met with teachers to better serve adaptive physical education students
   • Helped coordinated the Fine Arts Festival at Edwards Elementary

PRACTICA
Special Education, Ames Middle School, Ames, Iowa, Fall 2002
Adaptive Physical Education, Abe Middle School, Ankeny, Iowa, Fall 2002
Physical Education, Ames High School, Ames, Iowa, Spring 2001

COACHING AND ATHLETIC EXPERIENCE
Letterman, Iowa State Tennis Team and Big 12 Player of the Year, 2003
Club Coach, Tennis, University Club, Ames, Iowa, summers 2002 – present
Student Coaching, Ankeny High School Tennis Team, Ankeny, Iowa, Spring 2002
Private Coach, Tennis, Ames and Ankeny areas, 2000 – 2002

AWARDS AND ACTIVITIES
University Student Award for Volunteer Service, 2003
   (Volunteer service at Mary Greely Hospital, Boys' Center, United Action for Youth)
Member, American Alliance for Health, Physical Education, Recreation and Dance

---

References at Career Development Center, Any City, State 21345   101.555.0008

ALLI KATT

3 University Avenue, Any Place, State 21345 (101) 555-0009 allikatt@umiami.edu

TEACHING INTERESTS AND SKILLS
- Academic training in Biology, Physical Science, Environmental Science, Math
- Familiar with 4X4 and A/B block scheduling and working in interdisciplinary settings
- Collaborate with colleagues, parents, administrators, support staff, and area scientists

BLOCK SCHEDULING EXPERIENCE
Junior High Math and Biology, Community School # 22, Miami Public Schools, Fall 2004
High School Science, grades 9 – 12, Block Schedule Program, Fall 2003

- Worked in a high-school setting implementing a 4X4 block scheduling program (four semesters long, 90-minute classes per day). Developed lessons to fit the program. Incorporated various teaching strategies, including cooperative learning and hands-on approaches to science and math. Worked closely with team members in designing course descriptions and information packets for parents and other interested community members.

- Conducted practicum in junior-high setting using A/B block scheduling. Students enrolled for eight 80-minute classes, which met every other day. Effectively used various assessments and motivated students through an active learning environment.

FIELD EXPERIENCES
- *Spring 2003:* Student-taught in a science and mathematics magnet school teaching Biology, Research Lab and chemistry. Invited area scientists to present special lab sessions.
- *Fall 2002:* Participated in an elementary practicum, working in a kindergarten class 6 hours per week for several months. Worked on designing learning centers for science exploration.

EDUCATION
University of Miami, Coral Gables
- Master of Arts in Teaching, June 2004   • Bachelor of Science in Microbiology, *with honors*, May 2001

PROFESSIONAL ORGANIZATIONS
National Science Teachers Association; National Association of Biology Teachers

RESEARCH EXPERIENCE
- Research Assistant II, State of Florida Health Center-Miami, 2001 – 2002
Performed laboratory research in a microbiology lab studying the splicing of ribonucleic acid in Rous sarcoma viruses. Presented research (with team members) at regional and national conferences. Coauthored several articles in research journals and newsletters.

COMMUNITY SERVICE
Volunteer and cochair, Environmental Preservation Committee for South Florida
Fundraiser, United Way of South Florida
Builder, Habitat for Humanity

PROFESSIONAL DOCUMENTS
References and teaching (paper and on-line) portfolio available upon request.

Abe Sinclair

3 University Avenue   Any City, State 21345 (cell) 010.555.0009
abe-sinclair@uakron.edu   www.abeportfolio.uakron.edu

Teaching and Coaching Objective

Teacher: Middle School Social Studies   Endorsements: U.S. History, World History, Government

Coach: Cross-Country, Track, Basketball, Baseball

Education

B.A. Degree, May 2003   University of Akron, Akron, Ohio   Major: History   Dean's List

Student Teaching

Madison High School, Akron Public Schools, Spring 2003
   Ninth grade, U.S. History
   • Formulated numerous lesson plans for implementation into existing curricula
   • Constructed and taught an original unit on the women's role in the Civil War
   • Incorporated different teaching approaches, such as ability grouping and cooperative learning
   • Designed research activity using internet sources as well as books and periodicals
   • Encouraged historical inquiry through the use of political cartoons, propaganda posters, and primary
     and secondary documents
   • Revised classroom activities to accommodate resource and foreign exchange students
   • Participated in midterm evaluations and parent-teacher conferences

Practicum

West Magnet Middle School, Akron, Ohio, Spring 2002
   Seventh grade, U.S. History
   • Participated in an integrated block-teaching team comprised of 120 students
   • Designed and taught a lesson on the First Amendment using multimedia integration
   • Assisted in assessments, midterm evaluation and record keeping
   • Tutored individual students before and after school

Affiliations

National Council for the Social Studies; Ohio Council for the Social Studies; Geographic Alliance of Ohio

Related Activities

Rock 'n' Read Volunteer, Hobb City Center, Fall and Spring 2001, and Volunteer Coordinator, Spring 2002
      • Reading volunteer and tutor to inner-city youth
      • Organized volunteers and assembled materials for Rock 'n' Read activities and celebrations
University of Akron Cross-Country and Track Team, 1999 – 2003
      • Cross-country team captain, Fall 2002
      • Academic All-Conference Selection, Fall 2002
Summer Games Youth Camp counselor and weekend supervisor, Summers 1999 and 2000
      • Supervised youth grades 5 through 12 twenty-four hours a day
      • Facilitated youth activities, including sports, crafts, reading, and art

On-line teaching portfolio and credentials available upon request

Calista Woode

3 University Avenue, Any City, State 21345
010.555.0009 (cell)   cwoode@uisustate.edu

DEGREES	Indiana State University, Terre Haute, Indiana Master of Arts Degree, Special Education, May 2003 Bachelor of Arts Degree, Psychology, May 2001
STUDENT TEACHING	High School Special Education, Johnson High School, Terre Haute, Indiana, Spring 2003 Middle School Special Education, Horace Mann School, Indianapolis, Indiana, Spring 2003 Responsibilities of the above positions included instruction of mild mental disabilities–educable in a special class with integration and moderate mental disabilities–trainable in a special self-contained class. Assessed and evaluated the individual needs of students with learning, mental, and behavior disabilities. Designed and used Individualized Education Plan goals and objectives. Organized and implemented lessons in the four curricular domains with the main emphasis on concept development, language, communication, motor, and self-help skills. Worked with a special education team consisting of five specialists.
PRACTICA	Adaptive Physical Education Assistant, South Bend School, 2002 Life-Skills Training Assistant, Regional Services Office, Spring 2002 Behavior and Emotional Disorders, North Campus, Fall 2002
RELATED ACTIVITIES	Volunteer, Special Olympics Organizer and volunteer, Terre Haute Special Support Group Officer, College of Education Student Service Organization
PART-TIME EXPERIENCE	Weekend manager, Active Endeavors, Indianapolis, 2002 – present Clerk, Campus Book & Supply, Terre Haute (part-time), 2002 Receptionist, St. Mary's Admissions Center, 2000 – 2002 *(Financed college expenses through employment and loans)*
PROFESSIONAL AFFILIATIONS	Pi Lambda Theta; Phi Delta Kappa National Education Association; Council for Exceptional Children
CREDENTIALS	Career Planning and Placement Center, Any City, State 21345

J. J. MOA

3 University Avenue, Any City, State 21345   (010) 555-0009   jjmoa@uwyo.edu

DEGREES

Bachelor of Arts Degree, August 2003, University of Wyoming, Laramie
Honors: *Phi Beta Kappa, Dean's List, Presidential Citation, Buck Scholarship*
Associate of Arts Degree, June 2001, Casper College, Casper, Wyoming

TEACHING OBJECTIVE

- Speech and Drama
- Mass Communication
- Play Production
- Contemporary Literature

Qualified to direct play productions as well as small-group and individual drama contest events.

STUDENT-TEACHING EXPERIENCE

Speech and English Department, Albany School District #1, Laramie, Fall 2003
- Student taught an advanced speech course and a 10th grade American Literature and Language course, and team-taught an elective speech class
- Prepared educational objectives and lesson plans for three grade levels
- Worked with individuals, small groups, and large groups using various instructional and motivational strategies
- Supervised students in computer writing lab and special study-reviews sessions

Speech and Drama Volunteer, Albany School District #1, Laramie, 2002 – present
- Assisted with play productions and coached members of the speech team involved in interpretation events
- Traveled to meets, chaperoned, and supervised students

Middle School Language Arts, Big Horn Middle School, Fall 2001
- Assisted with lesson plans and progress reports
- Worked with three language arts classes during novel units; led small-group discussions and met with students individually

RELATED EXPERIENCE

Stage assistant, costume and scenery construction, University of Wyoming Productions
Actor, Wyoming Players Repertory Company (traveling company performing statewide)
Set designer and part-time actor, Big Horn Mountains Community Theater
Member and weekend supervisor, Gold Usher Corps, Wyoming Arts Center

PROFESSIONAL ORGANIZATIONS

Speech Communication Association
National Council of Teachers of English

Wyoming Communication Association
Wyoming Actors Guild

References Available Upon Request
Performance and Teaching Portfolio Available Upon Request

T. J. MEADE
3 University Avenue • Any City, State 21345 • 101.555.1111

OBJECTIVE   K-12 Substitute Teacher

EDUCATION   M.A. Degree, Developmental Reading, Fall 2003 – present
University of Texas at Dallas, Richardson, Texas

B.A. Degree, May 2003
Texas Christian University, Fort Worth, Texas
Majors: English and Elementary Education

Honors: Phi Beta Kappa   *graduated with highest distinction*

COURSES OF INTEREST

Reading and Writing Processes   Inquiry-Based Instruction
Supervision and Evaluation   Bilingual Education Methods
Classroom Management   Special Education Issues

EXPERIENCE   Student Intern, Wilson Middle School, Dallas, Texas, Fall 2004
• Responsibilities included teaching various units in sixth and seventh grades
• Participated in a five-member multidisciplinary team, including support staff
• Worked with a diverse population representing twenty different nationalities

Writing Tutor, Southbend Elementary, Richardson, Texas, Summer 2003
• Worked in the writing lab tutoring students with attention deficit disorder
• Maintained progress reports and communicated regularly with parents

Practicum Student, South High School, Dallas, Texas, Spring 2003
• Observed and assisted in ninth-grade general English classes

Composition Evaluator, Macmillan/McGraw-Hill, Houston, summers 2000 – present
• Evaluate eighth-grade compositions for the Indiana State Testing Initiative

ACTIVITIES   Volunteer for Youth Support Services, Dallas, summers 2003 – present
Asian Community Center Volunteer and tutor for immigrating adults, 2002
Member, National Council of Teachers of English
Member, National Association for Young Children

CREDENTIALS   Career Planning and Placement Center, Any City, State 21345
Telephone: 101.555.0008   www.careers.edu

HANK SPERRY

3 University Avenue, Any City, State 21345   (101) 555-0009
hanksperry@hotmail.com

**TEACHING
INTERESTS**

Technology Instructor
Expertise in computer science and electronics

**RELATED
INTERESTS**

Working with technology issues and related computer-based projects
Sponsoring student clubs and working with community groups

EDUCATION

University of Arkansas–Pine Bluff
B.S. Degree, Major: Computer Education, May 2003
Concentration: Middle School Instruction

North Arkansas College–Harrison
A.A. Degree, Electronics and Computer Technology, May 1995

RECOGNITION

Invited Member, Honors Program   Dean's List, 5 semesters
Electronics Union of Arkansas Scholarship   Chamber Award of Harrison

**FIELD-BASED
EXPERIENCE**

Semester Intern, Technology Lab, Pine Bluff Schools, Spring 2002
Practicum Intern, Middle School Electronics, Central Magnet School, Fall 2001
Methods Intern, Middle School Computer Lab, Pine Bluff Schools, Fall 2000

Responsibilities of above internships included:
- Planning educational objectives and lesson plans for computer technology and
  electronics units for middle-school students with a wide range of ability levels
  including non-English speakers and academically accelerated students
- Teaching computer-assisted instruction in various tech modules in a newly
  designed technology laboratory (Modules included hands-on applications in:
  electronics, transportation manufacturing, hydraulics, drafting, robotics,
  engineering, and multimedia productions.)
- Using various strategies, including cooperative learning and technology
  integration, with emphasis on goal setting and student responsibility
- Implementing positive and proactive classroom-management strategies
- Working in a team setting, attending in-service workshops and grade-level meetings
- Conducting parent-teacher conferences and student-led parent conferences

**RELATED
EXPERIENCE**

Tutor, Pine Bluffs Boys Club Volunteer Program, 2002 – present
Electronics Specialist, Arkansas Power Company, Little Rock, 1996 – 2001
Computer Programmer, Atlass and Stone Company, 1995 – 1996

**MILITARY
EXPERIENCE**

U.S. Navy, Electronics Specialist, 1990 – 1994
- Served on the battleships U.S.S. Missouri and Iowa

REFERENCES

References available upon request; portfolio at: www.avlon/hank-portfolio.htm

TONY STEPHENS

3 University Avenue, Any City, State 21345   101.555.0009
tony-stephens@hotmail.com
www.tony.portfolio.education.asu.edu

COMPETENCIES AND INTERESTS

TEACHING COMPETENCIES
Computer-Aided Drafting
Technical Drawing
Architectural Instruction
Construction Technology

SPECIAL INTERESTS
Head Coach - Golf
Assistant Coach - Basketball
Sponsor - Robot Technology
Advisor - School Booster Club

ACADEMIC TRAINING

Arizona State University - Tempe, Bachelor of Science Degree, 1996, Computer Science
University of Oklahoma, Norman, Teaching License, May 2003, Industrial Technology

INTERNSHIP

H.S. Industrial Technology, Flats High School, Norman, Oklahoma, Fall 2003
- Taught computer-aided drafting and design classes to juniors and seniors
- Taught drafting exercises, including dimensioning, sectional views, pictorials, and architectural floor plan design; provided tutorial services for students seeking advanced training
- Planned and presented units on using hand tools and basic carpentry for a one-semester Home and Auto Repair course
- Evaluated student progress by using various assessment instruments including pretests, posttests, rubrics, and skills-based portfolios
- Integrated advanced technical applications into lessons and robotics activities
- Worked closely with local business and community leaders to raise funds for students to compete in regional robotic contests

UNIVERSITY ACTIVITIES AND AWARDS

University of Arizona Golf Team, 4 years; MVP, 2 years, All-Conference, 1 year
Performed in numerous volunteer fund-raising efforts for local charities
Arizona State Athletic Scholarship; Dean's List, 4 semesters; graduated with honors

PROFESSIONAL GOLF EXPERIENCE

Tour member, Western Golf Professional Tour, 1996 – 2001
- Traveled with tour and placed in the top 15; qualified for the U.S. Open, 1999

Credentials at Teacher Placement Center, Any City, State 21345   101.555.0008

16

EXPERIENCED TEACHERS

MICKEY J. ROSE

3 University Avenue, Any City, State 21345   (101) 555-0008   rose@acnt.edu

OBJECTIVE

Teacher: Alternative-based education

Strengths: Individualized instruction
Goal setting
Advising and counseling
Conflict resolution
Community-based partnerships

CURRENT TEACHING EXPERIENCE

Teacher and Adviser, Alternative Center of Nashville, Nashville, Tennesse, August 2000 – present
Teach basic math, economics, computer science, and technology education to secondary
students in an alternative setting. Teaching and advising responsibilities include:
· Creating a classroom environment conducive to learning and appropriate to the
maturity and interest of the students
· Providing individualized instruction and counseling to students
· Supervising Center students throughout the campus and promoting consistent and fair
behavioral standards
· Designing and revising math, economics, and computer science curriculum
· Selecting with colleagues materials and resources appropriate for program's goals
· Helping to place students into traditional schools
· Giving regular technology training to all students using latest software/hardware
· Evaluating and selecting software in computer science and other curricular areas
· Providing training to staff for computer-assisted instruction and Internet applications
· Establishing and maintaining written and oral communication with parents

OTHER WORK

Paralegal Assistant, Smithe, Fords, and Jensen, Charleston, South Carolina, 1995 – 1998
Developed specialized databases for firm and client use to supervise and organize
logistical matters throughout all aspects of corporate transactions. Served as a resource
to attorneys and clients in researching transactions.

ACTIVITIES AND MEMBERSHIPS

Executive Committee, local chapter of United Action for Youth
Teacher Representative, State Advisory Committee on Adult and Community Education
Member, Tennessee State Secondary Economics Council
Membership Committee, Tennessee Association for Women in Computer Science

EDUCATION

M.A.   Exceptional Education - Florida State University, Tallahassee, Florida - May 2000
B.S.   Economics - Bethune-Cookman College, Daytona Beach, Florida - 1995
A.S.   Computer Science - Miami-Dade Community College, Miami, Florida - 1993

References and Portfolio Available Upon Request

C. J. CAMERO

3 University Avenue
Any Place, State 21345
101.555.0009   (cell) 345.456.1989
cj-camero@mail.com

OBJECTIVE	Art Teacher
ART EXPERTISE	Ceramics Painting Drawing Printmaking Sculpture Multimedia

DEGREES

Portland State University, Portland, Oregon
  Master of Arts in Teaching, Art Education, July 2000
  Bachelor of Fine Arts, Studio Art, May 1998

CLASSROOM EXPERIENCE

Visual Arts Instructor, September 2000 – present
Performing Arts High School, Portland, Oregon
- Magnet school operates year-round, with flexible hours; students represent diverse backgrounds
- Teach painting, watercolor, ceramics, and multimedia applications to advanced students
- Team-teach course in humanities and the visual arts for advanced-placement students in grades 11 and 12
- Developed optional after-school studio sessions and class review lessons in art history
- Supervise university students involved in semester-long internships and practicum assignments

OTHER WORK

Portland Visual Arts Center, Adult Division, 1998 – 2000
- Taught six-week courses in ceramics and basic drawing
- Collaborated with artists in dance to create original projects with integration and creative expression

CURRENT PROFESSIONAL SERVICE

President, Portland Academy of Fine Arts
Member, High School Fine Arts Curriculum Committee
Board Representative, Portland Arts Council
Grant Recipient, Fine Arts Partnership Project
Treasurer, Black Action for Youth (BAY)
Member, National Art Teachers Association

EXHIBITS

Juried Show: Portland Artist's Show, 2003
Group Shows: Seattle Regional Art Show, 2002
              Coastal Select Artists Show, Seattle, 2002, 2001
              Boise Group Show, 2000
              Midwestern Art Review, Chicago, 2000, 1999
Invitational Exhibitions: Vancouver Invitational, 2002

References available upon request.
Electronic art portfolio: www.cjcamero.pdx.edu

SUSAN LINN-GROVE _____

3 University Avenue, Any City, State 21345
101.555.0009   (cell) 103.553.0983
susangrove@k-12.mn.state.us

OBJECTIVE AND STRENGTHS

Teacher in an At-Risk Program
- Alternative Assessments
- Math/Reading Remediation
- At-Risk Population Experience
- Counseling Background

EXPERIENCE

5th/6th grade teacher, St. Paul Public Schools, St. Paul, MN, 2000 – present
- Teach children from diverse cultural and socioeconomic backgrounds in a high mobility school
- Employ manipulatives and alternative assessment techniques
- Coordinate parent/guardian at-risk involvement programs
- Work with students with learning and behavior disorders and use appropriate modifications and interventions, including behavior contracts and positive reinforcement
- Create original units across the curriculum, including hands-on math units stressing problem solving and technology integration
- Participated as a member of the district's writing committee and designed rubrics for math and science applications
- Implemented a "peaceable" approach to the classroom as a member of the Peaceable Schools pilot team
- Assisted other teachers with behavior modifications and interventions for students needing assistance as Student Assistance Team member

EDUCATION

St. John's University, Collegeville, MN
B.S. Math, May 1997   *with honors*
M.A. Education, July 2001

GRADUATE EMPHASIS

Behavioral Principles
Counseling for At-Risk Students
Assessment of Young Children
Interventions and Referrals
Adolescent and Young Adult Learners
Construction of Evaluation Instruments

AFFILIATIONS

National Education Association; National Council of Teachers of Mathematics; Minnesota Council for Talented & Gifted; Consortium for At-Risk Students

WORKSHOPS

"At-Risk Students in Today's Classrooms: Symptoms and Solutions."
   Region 10 Consortium, Atlanta, Georgia, March 2003
"Students At Risk: Reversing the Cycle of Educational Failure."
   State Educational Meeting, Jackson, Mississippi, February 2002
Conference sessions on topics of Reading Recovery and Literacy,
   International Reading Association Conference, Chicago, March 2001

REFERENCES

Career Advising and Placement Center, Any City, State 21345
Telephone: 101.555.0008   www.careers.edu

Jamie Hands

3 University Avenue, Any City, State 21345   cell: 102.555.0007
portfolio: www.jamiehands/teaching.htm

CAREER OVERVIEW

Business Education Teacher: 15 years
Yearbook Adviser: 10 years
Student Newspaper Adviser: 7 years
State and Regional Presenter: 3 years

PROFESSIONAL EXPERIENCE (16 years)

Laurens High School, Laurens, Arkansas, 2000 – present
• Business Education Teacher, grades 10 – 12; yearbook adviser
Frederick High School, Frederick, Oklahoma, 1992 – 2000
• Business Education Teacher, grades 9 – 12; yearbook adviser
Temple Junior-Senior High School, Temple, Oklahoma, 1988 – 1992
• Business Education and English Teacher, grades 9 – 12; student
newspaper adviser, assistant basketball coach

EXPERIENCE HIGHLIGHTS

Teaching responsibilities and course development:

Information Processing	Computer Technology
Business Calculations	Advanced Computer Technology
Accounting	Entrepreneurship
Personal Finance	Business and Contract Law

• Arranged for business internship opportunities and supervised student
interns
• Developed word-processing short courses for faculty development series
• Cooperating teacher for student teachers and practicum students

Committee leadership and responsibilities:
• Faculty representative, School-Community Partnership Coalition
• Planning committee, Laurens Parent Association
• Computer Needs Assessment Task Force, Laurens School District

PROFESSIONAL MEMBERSHIPS AND HONORS

Phi Delta Kappa, local chapter officer, 2001 – present
Nominated for Oklahoma Teacher of the Year, 1999
Outstanding Educator Award, Frederick Jaycees, 1997
Kansas Vocational Association

SELECTED PROFESSIONAL SEMINARS (2001 – present)

Desktop Publishing: Student Journalists	Methods of Alternative Assessment
Topics in Work Force Education	Technology for Restructuring Schools

ACADEMIC BACKGROUND

University of Oklahoma, Norman
Graduate Studies, Curriculum and Instruction, 2002 – present
Bachelor's Degree, Business Education, 1987

References Available Upon Request

RANDY BLANCO

3 University Avenue   Any City, State 21345   (101) 555-0009   r-blanco@smithacademy.edu

COMPETENCIES AND INTERESTS

Head Basketball Coach
Math Instructor
Physical Education Instructor

EDUCATION

University of New Hampshire, Durham, New Hampshire
  M.A. Degree, Exercise Science, May 2002
      Area of Specialization: Athletic Administration
  B.S. Degree, Physical Education and Mathematics, May 1994

COACHING STRENGTHS

- Motivate and develop all-around student athletes, physically and mentally
- Instill sportsmanship both on and off the court
- Possess thorough knowledge of basketball fundamentals
- Coordinate all program levels—elementary through varsity
- Initiate and maintain communications with parents, teachers, and administrators
- Work with summer camp programs and promote athletes to college recruiters

COACHING EXPERIENCE

Head Basketball Coach and Physical Education Teacher, Smith Academy,
  Bronx, NY   2000 – present
  Records and accomplishments:
  - Class 3A division; 24 wins, 8 losses (2002)
  - State qualifiers; district champions (2001, 2002)
  - Three athletes named to All-Conference Academic Team
  - Players selected on 1st and 2nd All-Conference Teams
  - Named Conference Coach of the Year (2001)

Shabazz High School, Newark, New Jersey, 1996 – 2000

Hayward Military Academy, Rockford, Illinois, 1994 – 1996
  Records and accomplishments for Shabazz and Hayward positions:
- Overall basketball record: 102 wins; 68 losses
- Honors: Conference Champions (three times), All-Conference selections,
  sportsmanship recognition, scholarships to Division I and Division II colleges

ATHLETIC BACKGROUND

All-Conference Selection, University of New Hampshire, 1990 – 1991
Most Valuable Player, University of New Hampshire, 1991
Selected for East-West All Star Game, 1991

CREDENTIALS

Career Planning & Placement Service, Any City, State 21345   (101) 555-0008

CARLEY CETT
3 University Avenue, Any City, State 21345   (101) 555-1111   c-cett@gbsd.edu

ACADEMIC INTERESTS AND TRAINING
Teaching Interests
Computer Science Instructor-Basic and Advanced Programming

Degrees
M.A.   Technology Education, University of Wisconsin-Parkside, June 2004
          Thesis: "Rural Schools: Teacher Training and Technology Implementation"
          Adviser: Dr. Will B. Proff, Chair, Technology Education
B.A.   Mathematics, University of Houston-Clear Lake, Houston, Texas, May 1995

CLASSROOM EXPERIENCE
H.S. Computer Science Teacher: Bay High School, Green Bay, WI, August 2000 – May 2002
- Taught students at all levels of computer knowledge, ranging from the novice to the experienced high school programmer
- Used various teaching and motivational strategies to encourage students to reach their potential
- Created a Computer Club, Senior Club (for advanced students), and a volunteer high school computer outreach team that visits senior citizen's centers to teach computer skills

Computer Lab Supervisor: Lakeview Elementary, Kenosha, WI, August 1995 – May 2000
- Supervised lab and instructed students from first grade through sixth grade
- Designed special activities to demonstrate basic computer concepts and usage
- Developed software to reinforce learning goals
- Taught districtwide faculty computer mini-courses and created a faculty computer resource center with ongoing instruction for grading programs, test development, and materials design
- Repaired and maintained all equipment

SERVICE ACTIVITIES
Pi Lambda Theta Member and Officer
Faculty Representative, Region 8 Technology Evaluation Committee, 2002 – present
Computer Programming Tutor, Kenosha and Green Bay, 2000 – present
Summer School Computer Instructor, Green Bay Summer Program, 2000 – 2002
Committee Chair, Green Bay Public Schools Technology Committee, 2002

AFFILIATIONS AND PROFESSIONAL ORGANIZATIONS
Wisconsin Technology Coalition for Secondary Schools
International Association for Computer Information Systems
National Council of Teachers of Mathematics
National Education Association

References: Career Center, Any City, State 21345 (101) 555-0008
Teaching Portfolio: www.cett.education.greenbayschools.edu

KEN DUITT

3 University Avenue   Any City, State 21345   cell: (102) 555-0009

EXPERIENCE SUMMARY	Driver education teacher: 4 years Physical Education teacher: 5 years Class advisor and coach: 9 years
EXPERIENCE	Driver Education, Joplin Academy, Joplin, Missouri, May 2000 – present – Provide classroom instruction, simulation instruction, and behind-the-wheel laboratory practice on the road – Deliver classroom instruction in basic and complex driving techniques and strategies, including personal and social responsibilities of drivers and inculcating safe-driving habits – Introduce driving simulator; supervise weekly simulator training for each student – Schedule and carry out behind-the-wheel instruction to provide observation and actual driving practice for each student Physical Education Teacher, Joplin Junior Academy, 1995 – 2000 – Taught skills courses including team and individual sports and fitness activities – Member of planning team to develop and implement coeducational Early Bird physical education classes
RELATED ACTIVITIES	Women's Golf – Assistant Coach, 2001 – present Volleyball – Assistant Coach, 1998 – 2001 Class Adviser, 1995 – 1998
PROFESSIONAL AFFILIATIONS	Missouri Education Association American Driver and Traffic Safety Education Association American Alliance for Health, Physical Education, Recreation, and Dance
SPECIAL INTERESTS	Tennis and Golf Classic and antique automobile restoration and repair
EDUCATIONAL BACKGROUND	Driver Education Certification Program, May 1999 Northwest Missouri State University, Maryville, Missouri Physical Education, Bachelor's Degree, 1995 College of the Ozarks, Point Lookout, Missouri
CREDENTIALS AVAILABLE	Career Center, Education Division Any City, State 21345 (101) 555-0008

LUIS CANTIUZ

3 University Avenue, Any City, State 21345
101.555.0009   (cell) 106.503.0922   cantiuz@mail.com

DEGREES

Master of Arts Degree, University of Virginia, May 2003
  • *Curriculum and Instruction with Literacy Emphasis*
  • *Literacy and Culture Certificate from Summer Institute,*
    Universidad de Seville, Spain, 2001
Bachelor of Arts Degree, Reed College, Portland, Oregon, 1996
  • *Elementary Education Major, Spanish Minor*

National Board Certification, 2002

PROFESSIONAL EXPERIENCE

Grades 1 – 3, departmentalized, cross-graded, team teaching
  Hanover County Public Schools, Ashland, Virginia, 1999 – present
Grade 2, multidisciplinary team member
  Goose Creek Schools, Baytown, Texas, 1996 – 1999
Teaching responsibilities of above positions include:
  • *Adjusting instruction to meet the needs of students in language*
    diversity, special education, and gifted and talented programs
  • *Using knowledge to develop meaningful learning experiences*
  • *Including assistive technology adaptations to allow students to meet*
    or excel in classroom activities
  • *Engaging students in various experiences to meet diverse needs and*
    to promote social, emotional, and academic growth
  • *Building a learning community by encouraging positive social*
    interaction and self-regulation for each student
  • *Communicating effectively with parents/guardians to provide*
    accurate data pertaining to student growth

CURRENT PROFESSIONAL SERVICE

Lead district in-service activities on Literacy Standards
Design literacy curriculum for primary units
Serve on the planning committee for Multicultural curriculum
Supervise reading clinic practicum students
Mentor university student teachers and practicum students
Conduct parent-education classes for the Parent Seminar Series

COMMITTEE LEADERSHIP

District Reading Committee, Hanover County
Hanover County Extended Learning Program Committee
PTA Faculty Representative—Goose Creek and Hanover County
Task Force Coleader, School/Community Collaboration Efforts

AFFLIATIONS

International Reading Association
National Education Association
Council on Effective Teaching
Virginia Association of Teachers

PORTFOLIO AND RECOMMENDATONS

Portfolio of teaching activities and teaching standards available
upon request or view at: www.cantiuz.portfolio/virginia.edu
Teaching references available.

TERI J. KING

3 University Avenue

Any City, State 21345   t-king@uiowa.edu

101.555.0009   (cell) 103.553.0983

SPECIAL STRENGTHS

• Collaborative team-teaching approach   • Multiage groupings   • Integrated curriculum

PROFESSIONAL CLASSROOM EXPERIENCE

Iowa City Community School District, Iowa City, Iowa

Longfellow Elementary-Grades 5 and 6, August 1989 – present

Team member responsible for leadership in mathematics for four-person unit teaching multiage classes, including SCI and ESL students.

Special responsibilities include:

• using cooperative learning, manipulatives (hands-on), and constructivist strategies
• scheduling planning to maximize blocked instructional and common planning time
• organizing and implementing special events in mathematics, language arts, social studies, drama, creative expression, and environmental education

Northwest Junior High - Instructor, Math Maintenance, summers 1996 – 1999

Team-taught math concepts on an individual basis working primarily with pre-algebra concepts; reviewed basic computational strategies; introduced new computer software

EDUCATION

The University of Iowa, Iowa City, Iowa

Ph.D. in progress, Curriculum and Instruction, 2001 – present

University of Northern Iowa, Cedar Falls, Iowa

M.A. 1993, Elementary and Middle School Mathematics

B.A. 1988, Elementary and Middle School Education

INTERNATIONAL EDUCATION EXPERIENCE

University of London, London, England

American Institute of Foreign Study Semester Abroad, Fall 1986

Oxford University, Oxford, England

International Student Leadership Program, Summer 1987

LEADERSHIP AND SERVICE

Longfellow Elementary School: Student Council Advisor, Safety Patrol Supervisor, Math Olympiad, Grade Level Unit Leader, Technology Committee, Scheduling Committee, Staffing Ratio Committee, Child Study Team, School Improvement Team, Phase III Committee, Building Handbook Committee, Conflict Resolution Training

Iowa City Community School District: Facilitator for Middle Grades Study Group on Transitions, Middle Grades Committee Curriculum Review for Media/Literature, Coauthor of Mathematics Scope and Sequence, Curriculum writer for Voyage of the Mimi I Literature Unit and Phyllis Reynolds Naylor author study

Professional: Presenter at National Council of Teachers of Mathematics Conference and Iowa Council of Teachers of Mathematics Conference in Des Moines, Iowa; Presenter at University of Northern Iowa Mathematics Meeting, Facilitator for Young Writer's Conference

Teri J. King
Page 2

SELECTED PROFESSIONAL DEVELOPMENT

Site-Based Shared Decision Making

Training included background of effective school research, development of decision-making skills, and overview of school improvement process.

Conflict Management

Training included planning for student and staff training, methods of record keeping, and program evaluation.

Study Group Facilitators

Training included the roles and responsibilities of study-group facilitators, as well as review of research on the effectiveness of study groups in the field of education.

Nonviolent Crisis Intervention

Training included nonviolent interventions for crisis situations in the classroom.

RELATED TEACHING EXPERIENCE

The University of Iowa, Iowa City, Iowa

Belin/Blank International Center for Gifted Education - CHESS Instructor
Math problem solving, summers 2002 – present

Private Tutor, Fall 1998 – present

Provide one-on-one instruction in the area of math and reading for grades 2–11

Graduate Assistant, UNI Mathematics Education Department, Spring 1989

Assisted with instruction of elementary mathematics methods courses for pre-education majors, provided tutorial assistance in math help sessions, assisted professors with research projects

Preschool Assistant, Chelsea Open Aire Nursery School, Chelsea, England, Fall 1986

AWARDS AND AFFILIATIONS

Kate Wickham Scholarship Honoree
National Council of Teachers of Mathematics
Iowa Council of Teachers of Mathematics
Iowa Reading Association

Iowa City Education Association
Phi Delta Kappa
Kappa Mu Epsilon
Kappa Delta Pi

References and Teaching Portfolio Available Upon Request

Nikki Solhisnsky

3 University Avenue · Any City, State 21345 · (101) 555-0009 · nikki-solh@fortworth.tx.edu

OBJECTIVE

Elementary Departmentalized Math Teacher

EDUCATIONAL BACKGROUND

University of Arkansas-Little Rock Little Rock, Arkansas	1999 – 2001	B.S. Elementary Education Mathematics and Science
Phillips Junior College New Orleans, Louisiana	1993 – 1995	L.P.N. Nursing

COURSES OF INTEREST

Calculus I & II	Organic Chemistry I & II	Physics
Linear Algebra	Anatomy and Physiology	Microbiology
Computing with Fortran	C and C++	Statistics

TEACHING EXPERIENCE

Stowe Elementary School, Fort Worth School District, Fort Worth, Texas, July 2001 – present
Classroom Teacher - Grade 2 and Departmentalized Math
Teach in both a self-contained and departmentalized classroom setting; use the methods of The Writing Process, whole language, and the integrated language arts; apply various math problem-solving techniques; field-test new math curriculum. Activities include: First-Grade Math Bee Coordinator, Social Committee Chairperson, Campus Coordinating Committee Member, Fort Worth Teachers', and Community Advocacy Committee Representative.

Amon Carter Jr. YMCA, Fort Worth, Texas, Summer 2001
Coordinator and Instructor of Live and Learn, a program for students identified as at-risk
Designed and presented life-skills lessons through group discussions, guest speakers, field trips, and active participation. Actively involved business leaders in the life-skills program.

Eisenhower Elementary School, Little Rock School District, Little Rock, Arkansas, Spring 2001
Student Teacher - Grade 4
Developed and taught poetry unit; instructed and supervised computer lab; worked with individuals in math; introduced and helped maintain daily journal writing; organized an all-school environmental awareness project.

Hoover Elementary School, Fayetteville School District, Fayetteville, Arkansas, Fall 2000
Practicum Teacher - Grade 6
Experience focused primarily on science instruction. Developed and taught science lessons; assisted with computer activities and individual work in math and science.

PROFESSIONAL-DEVELOPMENT COURSES

Classroom Management	Peer Coaching	Improving Student Writing
Quest	NASA Math	Newspapers in Education

PROFESSIONAL MATERIALS

Credentials: Available from Teacher Career Center, Any City, State 21345
               Telephone: (101) 555-0008
On-Line Portfolio: View at www.education.portfolio/nikkisol.htm

ADEL SHAKRA

3 University Avenue   Any City, State 21345   adel-sh@k-12.pa.state.us
101.555.0009   (cell) 103.553.0983

STRENGTHS

Creative Writing	Adolescent Literature	African-American Literature
Portfolio Assessment	Technology Integration	Journalistic Writing

EDUCATION

M.F.A.   Writer's Workshop, July 2001, Pennsylvania State University, University Park, PA
B.A.   English, Spanish, Journalism, August 1998, Temple University, Philadelphia, PA
A.A.   Computer Programming, May 1996, Valley Community College, Pittsburgh, PA

TEACHING EXPERIENCES

High School English and Journalism, University High School, University Park, PA, August 2001 – present
- Teach in a collaborative setting with 18 professionals. Plan cross-curricular units with science, math, and social studies departments. Use technology extensively to introduce new materials to students, to supplement traditional library research, and to teach basic layout design for newspaper and yearbook. Create and instruct units on early American authors, including minority authors. Conference with all students regarding writing and journal projects and final portfolio submissions.

Middle School Language Arts and Drama, Concord Middle School, Cranston, RI, Fall 1998 – May 2001
- Worked in a team-teaching unit with sixth- and seventh-grade students using block scheduling (90-minute periods on A,B schedules). Units on grammar, basic writing, and contemporary literature were designed by the team and supplemented with technology infusion, guest speakers, and cooperative learning.

RELATED YOUTH EMPLOYMENT

Youth Crisis Counselor, Campus Crisis Services, University Park, 2001 – present
Answer emergency calls, counsel and advice clients, and make appropriate referrals to college students and community-based agencies. Work with clients of all ages from teens to adults.

Camp Counselor, Camp Courageous, Mount St. Clair, Pennsylvania, summers 1998 – 1999
Worked with students with severe physical disabilities ranging in age from 5 to 25 years. Activities included horseback riding, boating and water activities, and crafts. Lived in cabin with campers and provided a comfortable, encouraging, and safe environment.

SERVICE

Committee Member, Technology Integration Team, University High School, 2002 – present
Presenter, Conference on Adopting New Technologies in Teaching Meeting, April 2002
Cochair and School Board Liaison to City Council, University Park School District, 2001 – 2002
Poster Session, Education Conference for Tomorrow's Schools, Cleveland, May 2001

PORTFOLIO AND REFERENCES

Portfolio materials and references available upon request.

MARY ELLEN DESMONES

3 University Avenue, Any City, State 21345
101.555.0009
mary-ellen@marion.k12.oh.us

TEACHING STRENGTHS
Recognizing and encouraging students who are talented to explore and discover
Working with teachers and parents to deal more effectively with gifted children
Teaching colleagues how to adapt learning materials for classroom use
Helping students develop a heightened sense of social responsibility for their talents

DEGREES
M.A. Gifted Education - Eastern Kentucky University, Richmond, May 2002
Elementary Certification Program - Ohio University, Athens, July 1996
B.A. Music Performance - Valparaiso University, Valparaiso, Indiana, May 1994

HONORS AND AWARDS
Awarded Outstanding Student in College of Education, State of Kentucky, 2002
2002 Governor's Award for Community Service
Smitson Scholarship for Music, 1990 – 1994

CLASSROOM EXPERIENCE
Teacher, Extended Learning Program, City Schools, Marion, Ohio, 2002 – present
Work directly with elementary students as an enrichment facilitator
Conduct student assessment, and provide in-service workshops for educators and parents
Work with teacher committees to schedule and coordinate school visits by speakers and visiting
    artists, and field experiences for large and small groups
Facilitate enrichment experiences for students interested in more in-depth exploration
Develop and conduct enrichment lessons and units, with particular emphasis on music
Participate in Extended Learning Program Advisory Committee

Teacher-Grades 4 – 6, Indian Mound Elementary School, Marion, Ohio, 1996 – 2002
Taught reading, language arts, mathematics, and science and music in grades 4 – 6.

RECENT PROFESSIONAL DEVELOPMENT
National Conference
Henry B. and Jocelyn Wallace National Research Symposium on Talent Development, Center for
    Gifted Education, The University of Iowa, Iowa City, March 2003

Presentations
"Identification of Gifted Minority Students," Conference on Gifted, Southern Illinois University,
    Carbondale, October 2003
"Gender Roles: Impact on Giftedness," Great Lakes Seminar, Chicago, May 2002
"Six Gifted Brothers: Family Ties," Governor's Meeting, Columbus, June 2002

References and portfolio materials available upon request

HEIDI WILKEN

23 University Avenue   Any City, State 21345   heidi-wilken@kc.k12.ks.us
101.555.0006   (cell) 103.553.0983

OBJECTIVE	German teacher (all levels)

COMPETENCIES	• Teach German to students at all levels in traditional and transitional settings • Design German curriculum for elementary, middle, and high school • Develop bilingual learning centers focusing on middle-school students • Contributing member to team- and collaborative-teaching programs • Create bilingual publications for school and community

TEACHING EXPERIENCE	German, grades 1 – 4 (2001 – 2002); German, grades 9 – 12 (currently)
	   Kansas City Public Schools, Kansas City, Missouri, 2001 – present
	German, Middle School Grades 5 – 7
	   San Antonio Independent Schools, San Antonio, Texas, 1997 – 2001
	Bilingual, Transitional Elementary Grades 4 – 6
	   Saint Louis Independent Schools, St. Louis, Missouri, 1995 – 1997

PEACE CORPS SERVICE	Science/Environmental Education, Senegal, West Africa, 1992 – 1995 • Trained teachers in rural schools on environmental education strategies • Organized pedagogy seminars and facilitated classroom exercises • Produced study manuals for students and curriculum materials for teachers • Coordinated education exchanges across the western part of Senegal • Built fences and other school infrastructure

COMMITTEE LEADERSHIP	Cochair, German Curriculum Project and Committee for Magnet Schools Kansas City Bilingual Consortium and Representative-Superintendent's Council

MEMBERSHIPS	Missouri Association of Teachers of German American Association of Teachers of German International German Student Society American Federation of Teachers

PROFESSIONAL DEVELOPMENT SEMINARS	Language Learning Centers for Elementary Students, University of Iowa, 2004 Midwest Regional Students-At-Risk Symposium, Washington University, 2003 Missouri Native Language Project, University of Missouri-Columbia, 2002

ACADEMIC BACKGROUND	University of Missouri-Kansas City, Kansas City, Missouri
	   Graduate studies in ESL and Bilingual Education, 2003 – present
	Black Hills State University, Spearfish, South Dakota
	   B.A. German and Elementary Education, 1992

REFERENCES	Available from Placement and Teacher Certification, Any City, State 21345 www.careers.edu 101.555.0008 (phone) or 101.555.0009 (fax)

MAGGIE HERNE-JOHNSON
3 University Avenue, Any City, State 21345 cell:101.555.0009
maggie-johnson@mail.com

TEACHING OBJECTIVE
Secondary mathematics with emphasis on advanced course work

CAREER OVERVIEW
Advanced-Placement Mathematics Instructor . . . . 5 years
Basic Mathematics Instructor. . . . . 8 years
Adjunct College Faculty. . . . . 2 years
Peace Corps Volunteer . . . . 3 years

DEGREES
Ph.D.   Mathematics Education, University of Illinois, Champaign-Urbana, May 2002
M.S.   Mathematics, California State University-Riverside, August 1988
B.S.   Philosophy and Mathematics, University of San Diego, May 1983
         Phi Beta Kappa

CLASSROOM EXPERIENCE
Advanced-Placement Instructor, Urbana School District, 1997 – present
Freshman Basic Mathematics Instructor, Chicago Public Schools, 1989 – 1997
Adjunct Faculty, Cook County Community College, Chicago, 1995 – 1997
Adult Education, Peace Corps Volunteer, Kingston, Jamaica, 1983 – 1987

- Classes taught in above settings include: Algebra (beginning and intermediate), Calculus, Statistics, General Mathematics Trigonometry, Finite Mathematics, Geometry, and Computer Programming
- Use Geometric Sketchpad, graphing calculators, and instructional software
- Incorporate national math standards into essential academic learning environment
- Collaborate with colleagues and contribute to local and regional academic groups

PROFESSIONAL SERVICE
Affiliations
Illinois Council of Teachers of Mathematics, member and former president
National Council of Teachers of Mathematics, member
Illinois Mathematics Education Association, executive board member
Midwest Mathematics Club, founding member

School Committees
Chair, Urbana Math Review Committee
Cochair, Urbana School Improvement Building Coalition
Member, Urbana School and Community Strategic Planning Board

CERTIFICATIONS, PORTFOLIO, AND RECOMMENDATIONS
National Board Certification; Teaching license in Illinois
Teaching portfolio available on-line at: www.teaching portfolio/johnson.edu
Teaching recommendations available upon request

CLARA PURR-WHITE

3 University Avenue
Any City, State 21345
(101) 555-0009
purr-white@mail.com

OBJECTIVE
Elementary General Music (K-6)
Instrumental Music (all levels)
Department Chair (K-12)

SPECIALIZED SKILLS
Aesthetic education studies and concepts
Synthesizer and audio technology
Classroom use of keyboards and guitar
Digital composing software
Supervision and evaluation of staff

CLASSROOM EXPERIENCE
Elementary General Music - 6 years
Department Chair - 2 years
Lake of the Forest Schools, Lake Forest, MN, 2000 – present

Middle School Instrumental Music - 3 years
St. John's Academy, Kansas City, KS, 1995 – 1998

School district committee service in above positions includes:
- NCA Evaluation team, Mission Schools, 2003 – 2004
- Curriculum development chair for K-3 music, 2002 – present
- Chair, Fine Arts Committee, 2002 – present
- Member, Districtwide Computer Committee, 2001 – 2003
- Faculty Representative, Community Advisory Board, 2000

LEADERSHIP & ACTIVITIES
Elected President, Minnesota Music Educators Council
Received Educator-of-the-Year Award, Kansas Academy
Supervised university student teachers
Wrote and directed two middle-school musicals
Produced several highly successful high-school musicals
Published "Electronics in Music Classrooms," *Music Educator's Journal*,
    Vol. 12, pp. 39–43, 2002
Served as Director of the Kansas Boys' Choir (Austria, Italy, United States)

AFFILIATIONS
Music Educators National Conference
Minnesota Music Educators Association
National Education Association

EDUCATION
Minnesota State University, Mankato, Minnesota
M.A. Degree - May, 2002   *Music Education and Theory*
B.A. Degree - August 1995   *Music Performance: Trumpet*

HONORS
Ken March Award for Talented Music Major
First Chair, Concert Band; Composition Award

CREDENTIALS
Career Office, Any City, State 21345 (101) 555-0008

CISCO MILES

3 University Avenue, Any City, State 21345   101.555.0009   cisco-miles@mail.com

TEACHING AND COACHING COMPETENCIES

CLASSROOM	*COACHING*	*ADVISING*
Physical Education	Wrestling	Class Sponsor
Health Education	Track	Homeroom Advisor
General Science	Summer Baseball	Rainbow Club

PROFESSIONAL EXPERIENCE

H.S. Physical Education/Health, East High School, Seattle, July 1998 to present
Responsibilities include teaching units in the following areas:
- Health-Awareness Issues
- Physical Education, all grade levels
- Co-ed Weight Lifting
- Physical Fitness and Weight Control
- Seminar on AIDS
- Nutrition
- Exercise as Leisure

Responsibilities include working as part of a collaborative team member using a 90-minute block schedule. Use various teaching strategies to motivate and challenge a diverse student population. Active participant in department and building committees.

ACTIVITIES AND AWARDS

Benefit Chair, Washington Heart Association, 2001 to present
Baseball Coach, East High School, 1998 to present; Wrestling Coach, 2003
Baseball Coach and Umpire, Spokane Summer League, 1998 to present
All-Conference Selection, Wrestling, Gonzaga University, 1996 to 1998

ACADEMIC TRAINING

Gonzaga University, Spokane, Washington, Bachelor of Science Degree, May 1998
Major: Leisure Studies   Minor: Health Education

Credentials at Center for Career Services, Any City, State 21345

JESSE GOLFE

3 University Avenue, Any City, State 21345
101.555.0009   j-golfe@mail.com

COMPETENCIES

Science: Chemistry, Biology, Environmental Studies
Technology: Basic Programming, C++, Java
Magnet School: Experience working in a specialized setting

PROFESSIONAL EXPERIENCE

Teacher, Technology and Science High School, Wichita, KS
1999 to present.
Teach upper-level science courses in chemistry, biology, and environmental studies to a multicultural student body. Teach vocational science courses preparing students for the world of work and teach advanced studies to college-bound students. Supervise students participating in internships with local businesses; hold regular seminars with corporate sponsors.

Freelance Consultant and Web Designer, 2001 to present
Construct Web sites for business and educational clients, including designing and customizing CGI applications. Provide training for clients to edit and design business Web sites. See Web site at: www.design.com

ACADEMIC TRAINING

Wichita State University, M.A.T. 1999, Science Education
Boston University, B.S. Degree, 1999, Majors: Biology, Math

CURRENT ACTIVITIES

Chair, Technology Department, 2003 to present
Council Member, Superintendent's Roundtable, 2002
Grant recipient, Environmental Studies Collaboration Project,
    2001 to present
Member, Collegiate Curriculum Review Committee, 2001
President, State Sierra Club, 2000 to 2001

AFFILIATIONS

Member, National Science Teachers Association
Member, Academy of Science

CREDENTIALS

Credentials: Career Planning Office, Any City, State 21345
Teaching portfolio: www.teachingportfolio/golfe.kansas.edu

ALEX ANTONIO–PONCO

Present Address
3 University Avenue
Any City, State 21345
101.555.0009

School Address
30 Royal Avenue
Mytown, State 23456
909.333.0003

TEACHING OBJECTIVE AND SKILLS

Social Studies Instructor; Cocurricular Sponsor; Athletic Coach
- Challenge and motivate students in a multicultural setting
- Use effective classroom management and discipline strategies
- Create and implement interdisciplinary materials
- Implement innovative instructional plans (community resources, case studies, simulations, field trips, computer instruction)
- Participate actively in team instructional and cocurricular planning

ACADEMIC BACKGROUND

University of Missouri-Columbia, Columbia, Missouri
Graduate Studies, College of Education, 2001 – present
Bachelor of Arts Degree, May 1995, Major: Social Studies Education
Dean's List, Daren Goode Undergraduate Geography Scholarship

CLASSROOM TEACHING EXPERIENCE

Hickman Senior High School, Columbia, Missouri   2002 – present
Pruitt Military Academy, St. Louis, Missouri   1995 – 1999
Summer Learning Program, St. Louis, Missouri   Summer 1999

Responsibilities during the above teaching positions include:
- Teaching courses in Geography, Latin America, World Cultures, American History
- Participating in daily team meetings to plan and implement interdisciplinary teaching units
- Working with English and Art in designing curricula for Latin American interdisciplinary materials
- Developing a prototype for districtwide portfolio for student academic assessment
- Encouraging parents to volunteer and participate in their student's learning activities
- Helping parents organize volunteer action groups and work with administrative teams

COACHING EXPERIENCE

Cross-Country Head Coach, Hickman High School, 2002 – present
Track and Cross Country Head Coach, Pruitt Academy, 1997 – 1999
Boys Club Track Volunteer Coach, St. Louis, 1995 – 1999
City Track Club Sprint Coach, St. Louis, 1995 – 1998
Three Conference Championships, Cross Country State Title, numerous all-conference selections, Conference Coach Award (2002), three sprinters invited to Olympic trials

COCURRICULAR EXPERIENCES

Academic Decathlon Sponsor, 4 years

Student Senate Advisor, 4 years

History Fair Sponsor, 3 years

National Geography Bee Coach, 2 years

International Club Sponsor, 2 years

Junior Historian Club Advisor, 1 year

COMMITTEE AND WORKSHOP ACTIVITIES

Interdisciplinary Committee Chair, Hickman High School

Social Studies Curriculum Review Committee Member, Columbia Schools

Site-based Decision-Making Committee Member, Hickman High School

Workshop Leader, New Staff In-service Training, St. Louis

NCA Evaluation Team Member, Blue Springs High Schools

MEMBERSHIPS AND LICENSURE

National Council for Social Studies

State Social Studies Council

Missouri and Kansas Teaching License

American Federation of Teachers

Missouri Historian's Council

Iowa Coaching Endorsements

COMMUNITY ACTIVITIES

Board member, United Way

Media Marathon Volunteer

Chairperson, Crop Walk for Austin

Fundraiser, Greater Columbia Crisis Center

American Heart Association

Troop Leader, Brownie Scout Troop #121

ATHLETIC RECOGNITION

All-American, Track

Team Captain

Most Valuable Player

First Team All-Conference

Academic All-Big Eight

MVP, Drake Relays

PLACEMENT FILE

Credentials: Career Planning & Placement, Any City, State 21345 101.555.0008

PORTFOLIO

Standards-based teaching portfolio at: www.portfolio.missouri/antonio

FANNY MENDEL
3 University Avenue, Any City, State 21345
101.555.0009 or 101.587.9054
fanny-mendel@mail.com

DEGREES

M.A. Special Education, University of Texas, Austin, June 2002
Thesis: "Community Mobility of Emotionally Disturbed Teenagers"
Adviser: Dr. Will B. Prof, Department Chair

B.A. Special Education, Emphasis: Behavior Disorders, May 1995

CLASSROOM TEACHING

Special Education Teacher, Alternative Center, Dallas, Texas, August 2002 – present. Case manager for emotionally and behaviorally disturbed students removed from local high-school programs. Duties include interfacing with outside referral agencies on behalf of students, coordinating the instructional programs, developing appropriate Individualized Education Plans, and designing and monitoring specialized behavior-management programs.

Special Education Teacher, grades 7/8, Independent School District, San Antonio, Texas, 1995 – 2000. Self-contained with integration classroom for emotionally disturbed students. Major teaching duties included reading, mathematics, and social studies. Implemented initial stages of the special education immersion program placing students in regular academic classrooms.

Special Education Assistant Teacher, North Texas Residential Care Center, Dallas, Texas, 1989 – 1991. Semiresidential placement center for emotionally disturbed students ages 10 – 18. Duties included assisting in all curricular areas primarily with behavioral situations.

UNIVERSITY APPOINTMENT

Supervisor of Student Teachers, University of Texas, 2000 – 2002. Supervised undergraduate special education student teachers in three school districts. Provided guidance to students regarding their instructional techniques and overall classroom performances during semester-long internship experiences.

RELATED WORK

Special Needs Assistance, Austin and San Antonio
Teacher for Austin Summer Program, Summers 2002; 2004
Planned activities for students ages 12 – 16 with behavior disorders.
Family and Child Trainer, Austin Community Center, 2001 – 2002
Provided 24-hour care for three severely/profoundly girls ages 4 – 6.
Direct Care Staff, San Antonio Haven Home, 1995 – 1997
Charged with the complete care of five severely/profoundly disabled teenagers in a group-home setting.

SERVICE

Poster Presentation: "Evaluation of Online Feedback as a Training Procedure for BD Students." Convention for the Association for Behavior Analysis, Phoenix, Arizona, April 2003.

Poster Presentation: "Alternative Settings for Success." Texas Special Education Conference, San Antonio, Texas, November 2002.

Portfolio and references provided upon request.

17

SPECIAL SERVICES

Keeler House ———————————————

3 University Ave., Any City, State 21345
(101) 555-0009
keeler-house@oregonst.edu

OBJECTIVE	Athletic Trainer

DEGREES

Oregon State University-Corvallis, July 2004
M.S. Degree, Athletic Training
B.S. Degree, Biology and Physics, May 2000
   Dean's List, graduated with distinction
   National Athletic Trainers Association member
   Oregon Athletic Trainers Society member

GRADUATE COURSES

Medical Supervision of Athletics
Biomechanics of Human Motion
Counseling for Related Professions

Contemporary Nutrition
Diagnostic Techniques
Clinical Sciences Seminar

TRAINING INTERNSHIPS

Trainer Internship, Capital Schools, Olympia, Spring 2003
Responsibilities included triage coverage of football team consisting of 120 athletes. Experience gained in injury rehabilitation programs, first-aid applications, fluid replacement, practice supervision, and facility maintenance.

Student Trainer, Oregon State University, Corvallis, 2001 – 2004
Responsibilities as a student trainer for various men's and women's sports involved in all aspects of the college's training program including diagnosis, treatment, and rehabilitation.

TEAM EXPERIENCE

Volleyball: Training Camp, 2004; Conference Finals, 2003
Tennis: Team Coverage and Oregon Invitational Meet, 2003
Football: Team Coverage, 2002; Spring Scrimmage, 2002
Soccer: Home Games and Regional Finals, 2002

REHABILITATION EXPERIENCE

Rehabilitation program involves treatment strategies, evaluations, consultations, and follow-up treatment for various sports. Observed three major surgical procedures for knee, shoulder, and ankle injuries. Special personal skills include swimmers' shoulder problems, ACL knee reconstruction, joint mobilization, and postoperative rehabilitation.

REFERENCES

Recommendations and training portfolio available upon request

ROXIE VALLEY

3 University Avenue, Any City, State 21345   101.555.0009   roxie-valley@mail.com

ACADEMIC BACKGROUND

Colorado State University - Fort Collins
   M.S. Audiology, June 2003   B.S. Speech and Hearing, May 2000

STRENGTHS

- Assessment of students using appropriate diagnostic measures
- Experience with a wide range of exceptional educational needs
- Adept at working with staff and parents regarding special services, treatment plans, and referrals
- Experience with adaptive technologies

COURSE HIGHLIGHTS

| Pediatric Audiology | Tests and Measurements | Remedial Methods |
| Clinical Audiology | Rehabilitative Audiology | Hearing Aids I, II |

INTERNSHIPS

Northeast Board of Cooperative Educational Services, Longmont, Colorado, March – May, 2003
- Participated in a program aimed at identifying students with hearing disorders, including kindergarteners. Selected and implemented therapy strategies for modifying communicative behavior of students with hearing problems. Participated in conferences with teachers and parents to foster communication and to develop appropriate intervention strategies.

Colorado School for the Deaf and the Blind, Colorado Springs, Fall 1998
- Observed and assisted with evaluation of children for hearing impairment, conferred with physicians, parents, and technicians about hearing aids or other appropriate treatment and therapy.

RELATED EMPLOYMENT

Colorado Lions Camp, Woodland Park, Colorado, Summers 2000 – 2003
- Residential counselor for hearing-impaired campers, ages 8 – 16; assisted with recreational activities, including backpacking, hiking, and overnight camping.

MEMBERSHIPS

American Speech and Hearing Association   Colorado Audiology Students' Association

References available upon request.

PIERCE GOULD

3 University Avenue, Any City, State 21345   101.555.0009   gould@uiowa.edu

OBJECTIVE

Counselor: Elementary (K – 6) or Secondary (7 – 12)

EDUCATION

The University of Iowa, Iowa City
  M.A. Degree, May 2003
    Counseling and Human Development
    Specialization: *School Counseling*
  B.A. Degree, May 2000
    Math and Spanish

**COUNSELING
SKILLS**

Provide individual counseling
Facilitate small-group counseling sessions
Conduct classroom guidance activities
Consult with parents, teachers, and community specialists
Coordinate outreach services to families
Use bilingual abilities to involve all students and families

INTERNSHIPS

Counseling Internship, NW Junior High School, Iowa City, Fall 2002
Counseling Practicum, West High School, Iowa City, Spring 2003
Responsibilities:
- Creating a positive and supportive school counseling climate
- Initiating conflict-management action groups for students
- Organizing before-school sessions for new students
- Implementing student-centered lunch seminars on topics dealing with coping skills, grief and loss, study habits, and health issues
- Incorporating peer-counseling skills into 6th grade curriculum
- Using various intervention techniques for at-risk students
- Maintaining progress charts for students on suspension
- Initiating and conducting parent/guardian-teacher-counselor conferences
- Working closely with mentor counselor in all aspects of the counseling profession (privacy matters, referrals, team staffings, administrative procedures, legal issues, and state mandates)

**TEACHING
EXPERIENCE**

Middle School Teacher, Los Angeles Unified School District, 2000 – 2001
Responsibilities:
- Providing leadership in mathematics for a four-person unit teaching multiage classes, including inclusion and English as a Second Language students in an urban environment
- Actively participating in curricular committees, parent-led initiatives, community-based programs, and student activities

AFFILIATIONS

American Counseling Association; American School Counselors Association

PORTFOLIO

Counseling standards documentation: www.pgould.counselingportfolio.uiowa

ROSIE WOODS

3 University Avenue, Any City, State 21345   (101) 555-0009   rosie-woods@waynest.edu

COUNSELING COMPETENCIES

Crisis Intervention   Group and Individual Therapy   Conflict Management
Multicultural Counseling   Chemical/Substance Abuse   Relationship Skills

COUNSELING EXPERIENCE

Crisis Counselor and Substance Abuse Specialist, 2002 – present
   King High School and Alternative Center, Detroit Public Schools
Middle School Counselor, 1998 – 2000
   Riverside Intermediate School, Dearborn Heights Public Schools
Crisis Intervention Counselor and Youth Advocate, summers, 2000 – present
   Youth Emergency Shelter, Detroit, Michigan

Responsibilities in the above positions include:
• Implementing crisis-intervention counseling programs and activities at all levels
• Collaborating with mental health and community agencies to provide services for students
  and families
• Coordinating with state and local programs in chemical abuse projects
• Developing various programs to assist students with personal and family crises

CLASSROOM EXPERIENCE

Journalism Teacher, Affirmative Action Liaison; Yearbook Video Advisor
      Ford High School, Detroit Public Schools, 1991 – 1995
Journalism, Drama and Debate Teacher, Peer Tutoring Coordinator
      East Catholic High School, Detroit, Michigan, 1990 – 1991

PROFESSIONAL AFFILIATIONS

National Counselor Certification Board
Association for Multicultural Counseling and Development
American Association for Counseling and Development
Michigan Association for Counseling and Development
National Education Association and Michigan State Education Association

EDUCATIONAL BACKGROUND

Wayne State University, Detroit, Michigan
      B.A. Degree 1990 Major: Journalism   Minor: African Studies
      M.A. Degree 1998 Counseling   Emphases: Counseling and Substance Abuse

PROFESSIONAL ACCOMPLISHMENTS

Rosie Woods
page 2

PROFESSIONAL SERVICE

2000 – present

Conferences Attended
Regional Crisis Intervention Consortium, Chicago, July 2003
Associative Disorder—Multiple Personalities Conference, St. Louis, May 2003
Michigan Conflict Management Conference, Detroit, November 2002
Association for Counseling and Development National Convention, New York, March 2001

District Activities
Chair, Crisis Intervention Curriculum Project, Wayne County Schools Consortium
Roundtable leader, School/Community Outreach for Youth, Detroit area agencies
Representative, Mayor's Action for Youth Council, King High School
Cochair, Substance Abuse Prevention Council, Detroit Public Schools

LEADERSHIP

National Delegate, President's Council on Substance Abuse, 2003
President, Great Lakes Regional Chemical Abuse Association, 2003
Conference Chair, State Crisis Intervention Workshop, Kalamazoo, 2001
Past-president, Michigan Association for Counseling and Development, 2001

HONORS AND AWARDS

Volunteer of the Year Award, NAACP, 2003
Blomberg Graduate Assistant Fellowship, 1998
Dean's List and Presidential Citation

Apple Award, KRNZ Television, 2002
F. J. Scotts Memorial Scholarship, 1997
Outstanding Citizen Award, Detroit, 1997

PUBLICATIONS

"Crisis Intervention for Families," *Intervention Newsletter*, Chicago, IL, 5(3), 2003.
"Substance Abuse and Homeless Students," *Journal of Substance Abuse*, Miami, FL, 8(2), 2001.
"Teenagers—Getting Your Attention the Hard Way," *Counselor Education and Supervision*,
    2(3), Alexandria, VA, Spring, 2001.

LICENSURE

National Counselor Certification
Private Therapist State Certification

State of Michigan Counseling Certification
Michigan Secondary Teaching Certificate

Maggie Love-Grey

3 University Avenue, Any City, State 21345
(101) 555-0009   love-grey@mail.com
Portfolio: www.love-grey.portfolio.education.htm

PROFESSIONAL SUMMARY

Media Services Specialist:	3 years
K-12 School Librarian:	5 years
Elementary Teacher:	8 years

AREAS OF EXPERTISE

Computer-assisted instruction	Computer use in learning resource centers
Evaluation of instructional software	Curriculum development
In-service programs for librarians	Program assessment of instructional software

PROFESSIONAL EXPERIENCE

Media Specialist, Hartford School, White River Junction, Vermont, 2000 – present
- Establish and maintain learning centers for computer-assisted instruction
- Consult with teachers planning assignments involving media and computer resources
- Evaluate, select, and requisition new print or nonprint materials and computer software
- Catalog print, nonprint, and computer software materials
- Assist teachers in selecting instructional materials
- Train and supervise clerical support personnel and media center aides

LIBRARY AND TEACHING EXPERIENCE

School Librarian, 1995 – 2000   Elementary Teacher, 1988 – 1995
International School of Beirut, Lebanon, 1988 – 2000
- Maintained library collection and sought funds to increase print and nonprint materials
- Collaborated with staff and international community to increase circulation and to promote reading in the classroom and home setting
- Taught social studies, language arts, and science for grades three and four
- Developed and maintained listening and writing centers
- Introduced computers into the classroom and taught students to use available software
- Cosponsored a summer reading project for all grades and subjects
- Active in committee assignments including Writing Process for Elementary Grades; Elementary Computer Committee to implement computer applications across the curriculum for grades K-6; Outdoor Education Committee; Superintendent Review Committee

DEGREES

University of Wisconsin – Madison
B.S. August 1996, Elementary Education
M.A. May 1998, Library Science

AFFILIATIONS

American Library Association
American Association of School Librarians
International Reading Association

References available upon request

ROCKIE BURRS

3 University Avenue, Any City, State 21345   (101) 555-0009   rockie-burrs@iu.edu

DEGREES

Masters of Physical Therapy, August 2003, Indiana University, Bloomington, IN
Bachelor of Science, May 2001, St. Olaf College, Northfield, MN

HONORS

Dean's List   Regents' Scholarship, four years
Johnson County Citizen's Award   Oake Achievement Scholarship

INTERNSHIPS

Orthopedics and Neurology Outpatient, Gary Medical Center, May – July 2003
Orthopedics Outpatient, Rock Therapy Center, Moline, July 2003
Neurology Rehabilitation Center, Trinity Hospital, Chicago, August 2003
> Internship responsibilities included evaluation, treatment, and progression of patients with various diagnoses; discharge planning; collaboration with other health care providers; patient and family education, and participation in in-service workshops.

ADDITIONAL CLINICAL WORK

Participated in clinics at facilities in Indiana (2001–2003) in the following areas:
- Orthopedics
- Sports Medicine
- Neurology Rehabilitation
- Pediatrics
- Spine Rehabilitation
- Acute Care
- Wound Care
- Cardiopulmonary
- Home Health Care

Major responsibilities and experiences included evaluation of patients with varied diagnoses, debriding and dressing wounds, assisting and encouraging patients with rehabilitative exercises and activities, gait training with and without assistive devices, and monitoring patients during exercise.

RELATED EXPERIENCES

Rehabilitation Aide, Bloomington Medical Center, October 2002 – April 2003
Physical Therapy Aide, Mercy Health Center, Dubuque, Iowa, Summer 2001
Residential Aide, Development Center, Chicago, Summer 2000
> Responsibilities in the above positions included:
> - Guiding patients through strengthening, balance, and coordination exercises
> - Transporting patients to and from therapy sessions
> - Facilitating the learning of activities of daily living, social skills, educational skills, and vocational skills among mentally and physically challenged adults
> - Performing passive-range-of-motion and assisted-active-range-of-motion exercises with residents

ACTIVITIES

Leadership Workshops and Leadership Mentor/Protégé Program
Biology Mentoring Program, three years
President, Lowden Residence Hall and Peer Review Team
Ace Bowling Volunteer and Wheelchair Challenge Committee Member

References Provided Upon Request

SCHOOL PSYCHOLOGIST

NORMAN TIPPIE

3 UNIVERSITY AVENUE, ANY CITY, STATE 21345
101.555.0009 (cell)   tippie@mail.com

DEGREES

Ph.D.   University of California – Riverside
Psychological and Quantitative Foundations/School Psychology, May 2004
Dissertation: "Intelligence Testing in Remote Settings"
M.A.   Educational Psychology, June 2000
B.A.   Elementary Education, December 1990

GRADUATE INTERNSHIP

Regional Center for Urban School Districts, East Los Angeles County, Spring 2003
Key duties:
- Administered and interpreted tests of intelligence, achievement, aptitude, and methods of behavioral and curriculum-based assessment
- Established goals and objectives to meet individual needs of students, including areas of substance abuse, social-skills training, therapeutic intervention, and parenting
- Worked with teachers to establish appropriate individual education plans
- Advised parents, teachers, and students on educational needs and coordinated services between the family, school, and other agencies

GRADUATE SEMINARS

Psychodiagnostics: Children and Adolescents
Consultation Theory
Behavioral Assessment and Evaluation
Individual Intelligence Testing
Assessment of Learning Difficulties

CLASSROOM EXPERIENCE

Classroom teacher, Rialto Public Schools, Rialto, California, 1990 – 2000
- Taught Grades 5 – 6 (6 years) and Grade 2 (4 years)
- Expanded multicultural curriculum, introduced whole-language approach to language arts and reading
- Developed learning centers for science and mathematics that were adopted throughout the district
- Served on district curriculum and textbook selection committees, and chaired teacher's association committees on welfare and negotiations

SERVICE

Volunteer Coordinator, Valley Crisis Center and Food Bank, 2003 – present
Executive Committee Officer and Board Member, Valley YMCA, 2000 – present
Past President, Valley Area Sunrise Rotary Club, 2000

CREDENTIALS

Career Planning and Placement Office, Any City, State 21345 101.555.0008
To view standards-based performance portfolio go to: www.tippie.us-edu.port

C. PENELOPE WYOMING

3 University Avenue   Any City, State 21345   (101) 555-1111   c-wyoming@ual.edu

ACADEMIC INTERESTS AND TRAINING

Professional Interests

School Social Work: Skilled in collaborating with teaching teams, parents and guardians, support staff, administrators, and support agencies

School Nurse: Expertise in managing patient care for special needs students

Degrees

MSW, School Social Work, University of Alabama, Tuscaloosa, Alabama, June 2003
BSN, Nursing, Texas A&M University, College Station, Texas, May 1997

GRADUATE COURSES OF INTEREST

Developmentally Disabled
The Adolescent and Young Adult
Treatment of Eating Disorders

Educational Measurement and Evaluation
Psychological Aspects of Adolescence
Advanced Seminar: Writing Approaches in Health

PROFESSIONAL EXPERIENCE

Graduate Internship

Collaborative Approach to Social Services Project, University of Alabama School Social Work Center, Fall 2003 – present

- Work as part of an educational team and provide diagnostic, direct, and consultative services for students in elementary and middle schools and their families. Work extensively with faculty mentors and medical professionals in reviewing remediation plans
- Work closely with local teaching teams, counselors, special education consultants, and administrators to identify students' emotional and learning difficulties and develop appropriate learning strategies and materials

Nursing

- Woodward State School for Adolescents, Mesa, Arizona, June 1997 – May 1999
- Worked in a team approach to manage the needs of severely and profoundly disabled adolescents; conducted physical assessments and collaborated with school staff and guardians

AFFILIATIONS AND ACTIVITIES

Member, Academy of Certified Social Workers
Member, National Association of Social Workers
President Elect, Phi Delta Kappa University of Alabama Chapter
Tutor, Northcrest Children's Resource and Action Center, 2003 – present
Special Olympics Volunteer, Alabama Council, 2003 – present

PROFESSIONAL EMPLOYMENT - MARKETING

Marketing Specialist, Nursing Associates, Mesa, Arizona, June 1999 – August 2000
- Worked on special accounts for hospital and clinics in the Southwest

---

REFERENCES: Career Center, Any City, State 21345 (101) 555-0008
PORTFOLIO: To view professional portfolio go to: www.penelope.socialwork.al.edu

JOHN RUNNING CLOUD

3 University Avenue, Any City, State 21345
(101) 555-0009   cloud@minnesota.edu

ACADEMIC BACKGROUND

M.A.   Speech Pathology and Audiology, *June 2003,* University of Minnesota -Twin Cities
Qualified to provide speech and language services in hospitals, clinical settings, schools

B.A.   Mathematics, *with distinction, May 2001,* Hamline University, St. Paul, Minnesota
Awarded Millers Foundation Undergraduate Research Grant

   Honors: *Phi Kappa Phi*
   Presidential Scholar
   Phi Beta Kappa

CLINICAL EXPERIENCE

Clinic: University Speech and Hearing Clinic, 2002 – 2003, University of Minnesota
Worked with patients who had articulation and voice disorders, cleft palate, and aural rehabilitation needs.
Hospitals: St. Luke's Methodist Hospital, Spring 2003, White Cloud, Minnesota
Department of Child Psychology, University Hospitals, Fall 2002
Involved in remediation for adults with neuropathologies of speech and language and children with language disorders; also worked with emotionally disturbed children.

PUBLIC SCHOOL EXPERIENCE

Practica: Elementary Speech Services, St. Louis Park Elementary School,
   October – December 2002
Preschool Hearing and Language Screening, University Speech Clinic, August 2002
Worked primarily with language-impaired and learning disabled children.

TRAINING ASSIGNMENTS

Research Assistant: Otolaryngology Department, University of Hospitals, Spring 2003
Researched language remediation in emotionally disturbed preschool children.
Instructor: Co-taught Clinical Procedures with Professor Vera Fine, Fall 2002
Presented lectures, worked with students, and was responsible for lab evaluations.

SERVICE

Memberships: American Speech-Language-Hearing Association, University of Minnesota
   Speech and Hearing Student Association (President)
Conferences: Attended American Speech-Language-Hearing Association Convention, Chicago,
   November 2003; poster session presentation at Minnesota Speech and Hearing Association
   Meeting, St. Paul, February 2002
Community Service: Cochair, United Way Fundraising, University Chapter, Minneapolis, 2003;
   Member, Citizens for Environmental Action, Minneapolis Chapter, 2000 – present

References available upon request

18

ADMINISTRATORS AND SUPERVISORS

HANK SPENCER
3 University Avenue, Any City, State 21345
101.333.0009 or 101.555.0888
hank-spencer@mail.com   www.eportfolio.hankspencer.com

OBJECTIVE
Department Chair – Social Studies Department

PROFESSIONAL EXPERIENCE: 14 years
Department Chair, Social Studies Department, Henry High School
San Diego Unified School District, San Diego, 1990 – present

History Teacher, Wilcox High School (grades 9 – 12)
Santa Clara Unified School District, Santa Clara, 1986 – 1990

Social Studies Teacher, Cherry Creek High School (grades 10 – 12)
Cherry Creek School District #5, Englewood, Colorado 1980 – 1986

EXPERIENCE HIGHLIGHTS
Participated in California Collaborative Teacher Intensive Training Program
Conducted new-teacher performance evaluations and tenure review sessions
Developed collaborative teaching projects among English and history faculty
Received state educational grant for advanced-placement course training
Directed the statewide Advanced-Placement European History Curriculum Project
Editor for a national newsletter for advanced-placement history teachers

CURRENT COMMITTEE LEADERSHIP
Member, California Committee for Talented and Gifted High School Students
Chair, San Diego Social Studies Curriculum Revision Project
Faculty Representative, Superintendent's Parent Advisory Board
Regional Consortium Delegate, State Department of Public Education 2004

PROFESSIONAL MEMBERSHIPS
Association for Supervision and Curriculum Development; Society for History Education
Council for European Studies; American Historical Association

ACADEMIC BACKGROUND
Stanford University, Stanford, California
    Ph.D. Curriculum and Instruction, 1992
    M.A. Medieval History, 1985
Santa Clara State University, Santa Clara, California
    B.A. European History and Middle Eastern Studies, 1980

SPECIAL RECOGNITION
Commencement Speaker (chosen by senior class) 1990, 1991, 1993
Governor's Award for Outstanding Work with Talented and Gifted, 1993
Appointed to President's Council on Learning, 1993
Outstanding Teacher Award, Stanford University, 1994
Selected for United Nations Middle East Study Trip, 1995

References available upon request at Career Planning Center, Any City, State 21345

K. C. PHOENIX

3 University Avenue   Any City, State 21345   101.555.0009
k-c-phoenix@isu.edu

PROFESSIONAL OBJECTIVE: ASSISTANT PRINCIPAL

INTERESTS AND QUALIFICATIONS

- Skilled at involving and communicating with teachers, pupils, and parents
- Knowledgeable about team approaches, multiage grouping, collaborative learning, and inclusion of second language students and students with special needs
- Expertise in curriculum, including subject integration, whole language, hands-on science, and math manipulatives
- Experienced facilitator for shared decision-making teams

EDUCATION

Master of Education, Elementary School Administration and Supervision, May 2003
    Indiana State University, Terre Haute, Indiana
Graduate work (14 hours) in Elementary Education Curriculum, summers 2000 – 2002
    Indiana University, Bloomington, Indiana
Bachelor of Science, Elementary Education, 1995, Bethel College, Mishawaka, Indiana

LICENSURE

Indiana Elementary Administration and Supervision License, grades K-6
Indiana Professional Teaching License, grades K-6

ADMINISTRATIVE INTERNSHIP

Oregon-Davis School Corporation, Hamlet, Indiana, Spring 2003
- Assisted with creation and implementation of student and staff schedules: 500 students, 75 staff
- Contacted and worked with parents to improve student behavior and classroom success; for final nine weeks assumed full responsibility, under supervision, for student disciplinary procedures
- Responsible for staff evaluation, reinforcing quality teaching, and fostering improvement
- Worked with a software consultant to design and implement a new district technology plan
- Organized and supervised extracurricular events, including student government activities, talent show, community-service projects, assemblies, and athletic contests
- Presented information to student and parents regarding expectations and programming
- Responsible for the editing and production stages of revised student handbook

ADMINISTRATIVE PORTFOLIO

Built on-line portfolio to document evidence of meeting state administrative standards.
Go to: www.education.administrative/portfolio.phoenix.htm

ASSISTANT PRINCIPAL (ELEMENTARY BACKGROUND)

CLASSROOM EXPERIENCE

Lincoln Elementary School, Gary, Indiana, Grade 6, 1995 – 1997; Grades 3/4, 1998 – 2001
- Planned and organized materials for thematic units, with extensive use of Reader's Workshop and Writer's Workshop techniques
- Developed and maintained an active learning environment, including use of manipulatives in math and science and collaborative learning strategies
- Initiated parent contacts and conferences to discuss home/school plans to enhance student achievement

COMMITTEE RESPONSIBILITIES AND LEADERSHIP

Grade Level Unit Leader	School Improvement Team
Scheduling Committee	District Management Team
Child Study Team	Building Expectations Committee (chair)

PROFESSIONAL DEVELOPMENT

Workshop in Shared Decision Making, July 2002
    Emphasis on team development, strategies for implementation, and facilitation
Conflict Management Seminar, June 2002
    Planning for student/staff training, program evaluation, records maintenance
Conferences Attended:
    New Administrators Conference, 2003
    National Administrators Conference, 2003
    Indiana Conference on At-Risk Students, 2001
    International Reading Association Conferences, 2000
    Young Writers' Conference, Oberlin College, 1998
    Indiana State University Conference on Students with Special Needs, 1998

SERVICE

United States Army, Microwave Radio Technician and Repairer, 1990 – 1995
    Support Company Soldier of the Month, December 1992 and January 1992
    Fort Ritchie Soldier of the Month, December 1992
    The Army Achievement Medal, September 1992 and May 1995
    The Good Conduct Medal, August 1993

REFERENCES

Dossier available from Education Careers Office, Any City, State 21345   101.555.0008

JOE LAW

3 University Avenue, Any City, State 21345
101.555.0009 (home) 101.555.0089 (office) joe-law@pa.school.edu

OBJECTIVE

Middle School Principal
Skills:
- Encourage parent involvement and participation in school
- Communicate effectively and build collaborative ties between school and community members and organizations
- Skilled in site-based management
- Accessible to all constituents

EDUCATION

M.S. Educational Administration, May 2001, Point Park College, Pittsburgh
  Thesis: "Personnel Selection Factors: Criteria and Process for Screening"
B.S. Degree, Physics, 1995, Cornell University, Ithaca, New York
  summa cum laude

Claremont Graduate School, Claremont, California
Scholar-in-Residence Summer Program, 2003
  Topic: "Educational Administration in Urban Schools"

LEADERSHIP EXPERIENCE

Middle School Assistant Principal, West Middle School, Pittsburgh, Pennsylvania
Major responsibilities 2001 – present:
- Directly responsible for supervising the computerized management system, including grade reporting, attendance, and records
- Responsible for student disciplinary procedures for 50 percent of the student body; also includes follow-up and parental conferences
- Conduct performance evaluations of the science and math faculty
- Supervise day-to-day instructional budget operations
- Work closely with the Allegheny County Sheriff's Liaison Program
- Involved with the Pittsburgh Center for Alcohol and Drug Services

TEACHING EXPERIENCE

Physics Teacher, Oliver High School, Pittsburgh, 1998 – 2000
Middle School Science Teacher, West Academy, Philadelphia, 1995 – 1998

ACTIVITIES AND AFFILIATIONS

Strategic Planning Action Team Member and Facilitator, 2002 – present
Vice President, Local Administrators' Action Team, 2002 – present
- Negotiation Team Member for Pittsburgh Administrators' Association, 2002
- NCA Steering Evaluation Committee Member, Oliver High School, 2001
- Pittsburgh New Schools Development Regional Member, 2000 – 2001
- Cochair, Site-based Management Committee, 1999 – 2000
- President, Pittsburgh Science Association, 1999
- National Association of Secondary School Principals
- School Administrators of Pennsylvania

References and portfolio available upon request

VERONICA KIRKWOOD

3 University Avenue, Any City, State 21345
101.555.0009 veronica-kirkwood@usc.edu

PROFESSIONAL SUMMARY
Assistant Principal .... 5 years
Intern and Research Assistant.................... 2 years
Teacher-International School..................... 6 years
Teacher-Stateside.................................... 2 years

AREAS OF EXPERTISE

Demographic Planning	Curriculum Development	Arbitration Agreements
Teacher Induction	Second Language Population	Database Management

DEGREES
Ph.D.   Educational Policy, University of Southern California, Anticipated May 2004
Dissertation Topic: "The Effects of Demographic Planning and School Participation"
Comprehensive Areas: "School Law, Language, Literacy and Culture, Curriculum, School Finance"
M.A.   Educational Administration, University of California-Riverside, July 2000
B.A.   Bilingual Education, California State University, San Bernardino, July 1988

EDUCATIONAL EXPERIENCE
Administrative Intern, Central Administrative Office, Riverside School District, Fall 2003
- Assisted in all phases of long-range demographic planning for the district. Projected enrollment shifts, boundary changes, staffing ratios, and transportation needs.

Research Assistant, School Consortium, University of Southern California, 2002 – 2003
- Researched and planned seminar topics for administrators. Topics included technology in education, sexual harassment and school policies, Americans with Disabilities Act, Family Medical Leave Act, blood-borne pathogens literature, and school emergency procedures.

BUILDING LEVEL EXPERIENCE
Assistant Building Principal, grades 7 – 9, Alvord District, Riverside, California, 1997 – 2002
- Member of four-person administrative team. Established a positive and orderly climate by opening lines of communication with staff, students, and the community. Encouraged parent involvement and participation in all school events. Worked with team to strengthen staff-development program and to increase monies for curriculum writing.
- Monitored school technology plan. Worked with technology specialists to develop student and faculty wireless computer stations.
- Primary administrator in charge of discipline; collaborated with Dean of Students.
- Evaluated certified staff including classroom observations, formal write-ups, and conferences.

CLASSROOM TEACHING EXPERIENCE
Instructor, Bilingual Training Program, University of California-Riverside, 2000 – present
ESL Teacher, Mentor Teacher, American School, El Salvador, 1990 – 1996
Bilingual Classroom Teacher, Jurupa United School District, Riverside, California, 1988 – 1990

VERONICA KIRKWOOD

PROFESSIONAL ACTIVITIES AND ACCOMPLISHMENTS

SERVICE AND LEADERSHIP
Committee participation
- Cochair, Graduate Student Advisory Committee, 2003 – present
- Graduate Student Representative, Five-year Program Review, 2003
- Chair, English Language Development Committee, 2002 – 2003
- Vice-Chair, Bilingual Curriculum Committee, 2001 – 2002
- Member, Student Attendance Review Board, 1999
- Member, Multicultural Curriculum Review Committee, 1999
- Member, Student Study Team, 1998
- Leadership Team Member, Program Quality Review, 1996 – 1998

In-service presentations
- "Monolingual Teachers and Bilingual Students: How Can We Communicate?"
- "Cooperative Learning Projects in the Bilingual Classroom"
- "Understanding Cultural Differences and the English as a Second Language Student"

Special projects
- Desert Cities Regional Reading Council
- Strategic Planning Board for Alvord United School District
- Community Parent Outreach Project
- School/Business Alliance of Riverside County

Recent conferences
- Annual Meeting of the National Association of Elementary School Principals, Orlando, Florida, March 2003
- Association of Overseas Educators, Indiana, Pennsylvania, Fall 2000
- Western Regional Meeting of Bilingual Educators, Provo, Utah, Spring 1999

SPECIAL RECOGNITION
Distinguished Teacher of the Year Award, California State University
University Graduate Thesis Award for Outstanding Research
Graduate Leadership Award, College of Education, University of Southern California
Undergraduate Achievement Scholarship, California State University

AFFILIATIONS
National Association of Secondary School Principals
Association of Overseas Educators
Association for Supervision and Curriculum Development
California Women in Educational Leadership

PROFESSIONAL DOCUMENTS
Dossier: Career Center, Any City, State 21345   101.555.0011
Portfolio: Standards-based online portfolio at: www.portfolio.veronicakirkwood.usc.htm

REGGIE S. PEABODY

3 University Avenue, Any City, State 21345   101.555.0009 (cell)
reggie-s-peabody@wa.k12.us

OBJECTIVE AND COMPETENCIES
Professional Objective
Coordinator of Special Programs

Competencies

Special Education Supervision	Compliance Monitoring	In-service Training
Psycho-educational Testing	Collaborative Consultation	Diagnostic-Prescriptive Teaching

EDUCATIONAL OVERVIEW
Special Education Consultant, 7 years; Education Prescriptionist, 3 years
Special Education Teacher, 5 years; Behavior Management Specialist, 2 years

CONSULTING AND SUPERVISORY EXPERIENCE
Educational Service Unit 31, Cheney, Washington, 2001 – present
Behavior Disorder Specialist and Special Education Consultant

Department of Defense Dependents Schools, Munich, Germany, 1998 – 2001
Educational Prescriptionist

Mississippi Bend Area Educational Agency, Bettendorf, Iowa, 1994 – 1998
Special Education Consultant

> *Responsibilities in the above positions included:*
> • Supervising special education programs for grades preK-12
> • Consulting with parents, administrators, teachers, and referral agencies
> • Coordinating with state and local programs in designing projects and writing grants
> • Providing assistance in curricula, program, development of individualized education plans, and preintervention
> • Assisting schools in compliance with federal and state special education regulations
> • Furnishing in-service training programs to parents, schools, and outside agencies
> • Giving psycho-educational testing and participating in interdisciplinary team staffings
> • Training staff in techniques for dealing with behavior problems in students

CLASSROOM EXPERIENCE
International School of Helsinki, Helsinki, Finland, 1992 – 1994
> *Behavior Disorders and Learning Disabilities Teacher*
> Senior Class Advisor; Sophomore Girls' Basketball Coach
> Mentor Teacher

Cooperative Education Service Unit, Elm Grove, Wisconsin, 1991 – 1992
> *Secondary Special Education Multidisability Resource Teacher*
> Faculty Advisor to Students Against Drunk Driving Club

Kauai School District, Waimea, Kauai, 1990 – 1991
> *Behavior Specialist and In-School Suspension Teacher*
> Intramural Director
> Chess Club Advisor

DEGREES
University of Hawaii-Manoa, Honolulu, Hawaii
Bachelor of Science Degree, 1986   Special Education
Master of Arts Degree, 1990   Behavior Disorders
Educational Specialist Degree, 1998   Educational Administration

Additional special education graduate course work completed at
University of Washington, Seattle
Michigan State University - Summer Campus, Cyprus
Iowa State University, Ames

LICENSURE
Wisconsin dual licensure in Emotional/Behavior Disabilities and Learning Disabilities
Iowa and Washington Supervisory (K-12) Special Education Certificates
Washington licensure in Emotional/Behavior, and General Special Education

CURRENT PROFESSIONAL ACTIVITIES
Training sessions
"Orientation Programs and New Staff Success," staff training sessions presented at six regional centers in Oregon and Washington, 2002 – present

"Quality Assurance/Peer Review Programs," supervisory training sessions offered for referral agencies and special education service units in Washington, 2002 – 2003

"Understanding and Monitoring Rules and Regulations with Third-Party Systems," in-house training sessions for directors of various departments, Cheney, Washington, 2001 – 2002

Committees
Chair, Northwest Regional Special Education Staff Consortium
Chair, Orientation Review Committee, Educational Service Unit I
Member, Computerized Special Education Resources Inventory System

INTERNATIONAL INTERESTS
• International study in England, Germany, France, and Cyprus
• Cofounder, ASIA Outreach Program, Cheney, Washington
• Host Family, Foreign Field Service Students
• Member, International Woman's Club
• Volunteer, AmeriCares Association

MILITARY SERVICE
United States Air Force, Second Lieutenant - Air Borne Division, 1974 – 1978
Awarded commendations for flight training and flight performance, 3 years

PROFESSIONAL AFFILIATIONS
Association for Overseas Educators
American Association for Curriculum and Development
National Association of Supervisors and Directors of Secondary Education

Dossier and Standards-Based Portfolio Available Upon Request

IMA FINE
3 University Avenue, Any City, State 21345
(101) 555-0009   ima-fine@mail.com

PROFESSIONAL OBJECTIVE
Human Resources Director

ADMINISTRATIVE STRENGTHS
- Provide leadership for planning, coordinating, supervising, and evaluating all personnel services, including recruitment, selection, and assignment of staff
- Strong knowledge of state and federal guidelines and legislation (Americans with Disabilities Act, Affirmative Action, Civil Rights Act, Age Discrimination) regarding hiring practices and selection procedures
- Experience in shared decision-making and site-based management practices
- Able to collaborate with management, the Board of Education, professional and support staff, students, parents, and community
- Experience in systemwide information management and databased decision making

EDUCATIONAL EXPERIENCE SUMMARY
Graduate Research Assistant, University of Nebraska, 2000 – 2003
Director of Personnel, Omaha Public Schools, Omaha, 1995 – 2000
Coordinator of Curriculum and Instruction, Bering Strait, Alaska, 1993 – 1995
Language Arts/Chapter One Coordinator, Baltimore, Maryland, 1990 – 1992
Secondary English Teacher, Agana, Guam, 1988 – 1990

DEGREES
Ph.D.   **Planning, Policy, and Leadership Studies,** University of Nebraska-Lincoln, May 2003
Dissertation Topic: "Analysis of Prescribed Interview Styles and Candidate Ranking"

M.A.   **Mass Communication,** Johns Hopkins University, Baltimore, Maryland, June 1993
Emphasis: Institutional Public Relations

B.S.   **English and Mass Communication,** University of Guam, Mangilao, Guam, May 1988
Phi Beta Kappa   *graduated with highest distinction*

SPECIAL RECOGNITION
Teaching Assistant of the Year Award, University of Nebraska, 2003
Simmons Medallion for Leadership in Academics, University of Nebraska, 2003

GRADUATE ASSISTANTSHIPS
Research Assistant, Institute for School Executives, College of Education, University of Nebraska, 2001 – 2003. Assisted with the planning and organization of four major institutes per year. Invited renowned speakers from across the nation to address school administrators from across the state. Participated in preparation of a grant funded by the Geraldine Dodge Foundation.

Supervisor of Student Teachers, College of Education, University of Nebraska, 2000 – 2002. Supervised, advised, and evaluated 13 secondary student teachers. Worked with public school teachers and administrators in various settings. Presented workshops on classroom management, instructional strategies, and salary negotiations.

PROFESSIONAL EXPERIENCE
Director of Personnel, Omaha Public Schools, Omaha, Nebraska, 1995 – 2000
- Planned and revised personnel management regulations in accordance with Board policy
- Organized effective and appropriate procedures to recruit, select, and retain quality staff
- Monitored the ongoing success of the district's personnel efforts and supervised staff
- Implemented a minority-recruitment process, including the planning of recruitment trips, compilation of data, screening, interviewing, and maintenance of records
- Developed staffing plans and recommended teaching assignments and districtwide transfers
- Assisted in staff reductions, terminations, and recall proceedings

Coordinator of Curriculum and Instruction, Bering Strait Schools, Unalakleet, 1993 – 1995
- Worked cooperatively with staff and administrators on curriculum issues in 16 villages spanning 80,000 square miles of rugged terrain
- Facilitated major revision of intermediate curriculum, replacing current programs with integrated and developmentally appropriate practices
- With staff collaboration, developed a state recognized K-8 literacy program
- Established a business/school partnership to create wireless computer labs
- Designed intensive staff-development plan to support curricular change

Language Arts/Chapter I Coordinator, St. John's Academy, Baltimore, Maryland, 1990 – 1992
- Organized and directed K-12 services in reading and language arts
- Worked with staff to implement process writing, whole language methodology, reading in the content areas, children's literature, alternative assessment, thinking-skills infusion, and multiple intelligence theory
- Developed action teams to include staff at all levels

Secondary English Teacher, Washington High School, Agana, Guam, 1988 – 1990
- Taught English 9, Honors 10, Journalism and Publications, and Creative Writing, an elective class offered through after-school and extended-learning programs. Served as advisor of the school newspaper, *The Banana Leaf.*

RECENT SEMINARS AND CONFERENCES
State Leadership Conference, School Administrators Plains Meeting, Denver, October 2002
AASPA Symposium on Management Innovations, San Diego, California, July 2002
AASPA National Convention, Leadership Series for Women, Washington, D.C., October 2001
Alaska Association for Bilingual Education, Fairbanks, Alaska, June 2000
Iowa Language Arts Conference (invited speaker), Drake University, Des Moines, May 2000
Northwest Regional States Conference on Outcome Based Education, Seattle, March 2000

References provided upon request.

HIREM E. SOON

3 University Avenue, Any City, State 21345   hiremesoon@ca.sm.edu
101.555.0009 (cell)   101.555.8888 (work)

ACADEMIC PREPARATION

Ph.D. **Policy and Leadership Studies, May 2001**
University of California-Berkeley
Dissertation: "Cultural Comparisons of Urban Education"
Advisor: Bea Fine, Ph.D.
Awarded *Outstanding Dissertation* by Phi Delta Kappa

M.A. **Educational Administration, May 1992**
Rice University, Houston, Texas
Thesis "Interdisciplinary Models: Urban Schools That Succeed"

B.S. **German Studies and History, December 1985**
Texas A&M University, College Station, Texas
with highest distinction

K-12 EXPERIENCE

Superintendent of Schools, Long Beach District 28, July 2001 – present
Enrollment and staff: 12,900 students, 545 certified staff, 200 classified staff, 38 licensed administrators. Budget: 100.4 million; successful bond referendum: 18.8 million for new year-round high school

Assistant Superintendent, 1998 – 1999; High School Principal, 1994 – 1998; Assistant High School Principal, 1992 – 1994, Riverside Public Schools, Riverside, California

Classroom Teacher, German and History, 1985 – 1989, Clark County Schools, Las Vegas, Nevada (2 years); Edgewood Independent School District, San Antonio, Texas (2 years)

RELATED LEADERSHIP AND RESEARCH ACTIVITIES

West Coast Educational Research Grant, National Urban Youth Coalition, 2002 – present
In collaboration with UC faculty, was awarded grant ($550,000) to initiate urban learning centers. Working in cooperation with state education leaders, teachers, business and community leaders to design centers that prepare urban students for workforce success.

Graduate Research Assistant, Policy Studies, UC-Berkeley Graduate School, 2000
Under the direction of Professor Reed A. Lott, collected, reviewed, and analyzed the early school restructuring movement. Developed a bibliography for use in the course *School Reformation*. Bibliography incorporated into the index of the *Policy Leadership Handbook* edited by Dr. Lott.

Fulbright Scholar Program Research Award, Bucharest, Romania, 1999 – 2000
In consultation with Romanian education officials, studied school curricula and state-mandated materials with a special emphasis on technology. Reviewed government archives and worked closely with Romanian postsecondary instructors to examine curriculum resources.

PROFESSIONAL SERVICE
(1998 – present)

Leadership
Representative, California Governor's Commission on Secondary Schools, 2003 – present
Conference Chair, Western Regional Educational Association, Los Angeles, October, 2003
Board Member, State of California Economic Development Growth Commission, 2002 – 2003
President (1997) and Charter Member, Urban Schools Coalition, Los Angeles, 2000 – 2003

Presentations
"Restructuring = Total Commitment," State Governor's Forum, Oakland, California, March 2003
"Involving Parents in School Programs," School Administrators Conference, Stanford, May 2002
"Partnerships with Real Results," American School Administrators Meeting, Atlanta, May 2002
"Telecommunications: Tools for Reform," West School Boards Conference, Phoenix, July 2001
"Global Learning Communities," New Schools Coalition Meeting, Detroit, October 2001
"Designing Schools for Success," National Education Association Convention, Detroit, April 1999
"Technology and Urban School Reform," NEA National Conference Series, Tampa, June 1992

Publications
Bare, A.J. and Dunne, I.M. "Demystifying Reform," *Learning Magazine,* 4, 2 (May 2002): 17
Bare, A.J. "One Approach to School Reform," *West Curriculum Bulletin,* XI, 3 (Fall 2001): 7–9

Partnerships and Grants
Technology Grant, West Coast Partnership Inc., Los Angeles, California, 2002 – present
Working in partnership with staff, university and local corporate leaders in developing state-of-the-art technology labs in K-12 buildings. Designing a shared professionals exchange to use the expertise of business leaders in classrooms; teachers provide enrichment courses at business site.

Coastal Project Block Grant, Los Angeles County Business School Partnership, 2002
Initiated and led the design and development of two new learning centers that incorporated performance-based learning goals, year-round, evening and flexible hours, integrated course work, technology infusion, teaching teams, and community advisory boards.

Memberships
American Association of School Administrators	New Schools Coalition
California Association of School Administrators	National Education Association
West Coast Regional Association	National Alliance of Black Educators

Community Activism
Commission member, Youth 2004, Los Angeles County; Elected to Board of Directors, 2002
President (2001) and member of Southern California Youth Action Committee, 2000 – present
Chair, Chamber of Commerce Futures Committee, Los Angeles Chamber of Commerce, 2000 – present
Volunteer Big Brother, Southside Los Angeles Big Brother, Inc., 1998 – present

References and Administrative Portfolio Available Upon Request

HIREM E. SOON

3 University Avenue, Any City, State 21345   hiremesoon@ca.sm.edu
101.555.0009 (cell)   101.555.8888 (work)

ACADEMIC PREPARATION

Ph.D.   **Policy and Leadership Studies, May 2001**
       University of California-Berkeley

M.A.   **Educational Administration, May 1992**
       Rice University, Houston, Texas

B.S.   **German Studies and History, December 1985**
       Texas A&M University, College Station, Texas
       with highest distinction

PROFESSIONAL EXPERIENCE SUMMARY

Superintendent of Schools, Long Beach District 28, July 2001 – present
Assistant Superintendent, Principal/Assistant Principal, 1992 – 1999, Riverside, California
Classroom Teacher, German/History, 1985 – 1989, Las Vegas, Nevada and San Antonio, Texas

RELATED LEADERSHIP AND RESEARCH ACTIVITIES

West Coast Educational Research Grant, National Coalition for Urban Youth, 2002 – present
Graduate Research Assistant, Policy Leadership Studies, UC-Berkeley Graduate School, 2000
Fulbright Scholar Program-Research Award, Bucharest, Romania, 1999 – 2000

SERVICE

Leadership
- Representative, California Governor's Commission on Secondary Schools, 2003 – present
- Conference Chair, Western Regional Educational Association, Los Angeles, October, 2003
- Board Member, State of California Economic Development Growth Commission, 2002 – 2003
- President (2001) and Charter Member, Urban Schools Coalition, Los Angeles, 2000 – 2003

Presentations and Publications
- "Restructuring = Total Commitment," State Governor's Forum, Oakland, California, March 2003
- "Involving Parents in School Programs," School Administrators Conference, Stanford, May 2002
- "Partnerships with Real Results," American School Administrators Meeting, Atlanta, May 2002
- Bare, A.J. and Dunne, I.M. "Demystifying Reform," *Learning Magazine,* 4, 2 (May 2002): 17
- Bare, A.J. "One Approach to School Reform," *West Curriculum Bulletin,* XI, 3 (Fall 2001): 7–9

Partnership Projects
- Technology Grant, West Coast Partnership Inc., Los Angeles, California, 2002 – present
- Coastal Project Block Grant, Los Angeles County Business School Partnership, 2002

Community Activism
- Commission member, Youth 2004, Los Angeles County; Elected to Board of Directors, 2002
- President (2001) and member of Southern California Youth Action Committee, 2000 – present
- Chair, Chamber of Commerce Futures Committee, Los Angeles Chamber of Commerce, 2000
- Volunteer Big Brother, Southside Los Angeles Big Brother, Inc., 1998 – present

Complete list of publications, presentations, and service available upon request

19

SECOND CAREER OR NONLICENSED INDIVIDUALS

(Designed for individuals who do not currently hold a teaching license.)

Amanda R. Arnott

3 University Avenue, Any City, State 21345   101.555.0008   arnott@ak.edu

Objective
Elementary teacher in a bilingual setting

Education

University of Arkansas, Fayetteville	Bachelor of Arts Degree, May 2002
Walter J. Lemke Department of Journalism	Majors: Public Relations, Advertising, Spanish
Minors: Psychology, Political Science	Cumulative GPA: 3.86/4.00

Special Recognition and Honors
National Society of Collegiate Scholars Honor Society
Golden Key Honor Society
Gamma Beta Phi Honor Society
NSCS delegate nomination to 2002 International Mission on Diplomacy
University of Arkansas Study Abroad Scholarship
Panhellenic Outstanding Achievement Recognition

Technology Skills

Adobe Illustrator	Internet Applications
Microsoft Office	QuarkXPress

International Study
University of Kansas Summer Institute in Barcelona, Catalonia, Spain, 2001
Successfully completed courses in Spanish grammar, composition, and conversation

Professional Experience
Client Service Representative, Adell Communications, Little Rock, Arkansas, June 2002 – present

Leadership and Service
President of the Associated Student Government Freshman Senators, Fall 1999
Organized a training session for incoming senators

Psychology Research Assistant, Spring 1999 – Spring 2000
Conducted and analyzed research findings; assisted in compiling material for publication; awarded poster acceptance to American Psychological Society Convention in Miami

University Programs Performing Arts Committee Hospitality Director, 1998 – 1999
Facilitated in negotiating contracts for performers; scheduled publicity and catering for the events; coordinated lodging and transportation for the entertainers

Campus Activities
Public Relations Student Society of America; Arkansas Razorback Booster Club
University of Arkansas Commission 2010 Consulting Board
Salvation Army/Arkansas Children's Hospital Volunteer

References:	Available upon request
Portfolio:	Writing samples and documentation of skills and abilities available upon request

April Moon

3 University Avenue, Any City, State 21345
april-moon@mail.com   102.555.0007 cell

OBJECTIVE

Teacher: Elementary-age students in a multicultural environment
Sponsor: Collaborate in school productions in music, drama, or art

STRENGTHS

- Have developed strong communication skills and am adept at working with people of all ages in various situations
- Well-organized leader who can successfully function in high stress situations
- Able to establish a community and design, implement, and manage programs with youth
- Willing to try new experiences and open my mind to broaden world perspective

WORK EXPERIENCE

Technical Assistant, Ogunquit Playhouse, Ogunquit, Maine, summers 2001 and 2002
    Worked with a skilled team to construct, paint, and execute summer stock performances.
Community Development Professional, Kumanovo, Macedonia, September 1988 – May 2001
    Organized and led grassroots community educational programs and multicultural, integrated education in a time of civil unrest. Taught English, Model United Nations, and economics to high-school and adult students. Designed and implemented an English language camp and a Girls Leading our World (GLOW) symposium.

VOLUNTEER EXPERIENCE

Crisis Center: Intensively trained to volunteer weekly, for three years, helping with counseling and suicide intervention. Selected to be a mentor for new volunteers.

Free Lunch Program: Collaborated with other community members to help feed the hungry.

Tutor for English as a Foreign Language: Worked with graduate students at the University Speaking Lab.

Friendly Farm: Fostered skills about producing, maintaining, and distributing organic foods.

ACADEMIC BACKGROUND

B.A. Degree, University of New England, Biddeford, Maine, December 1997
    Major: Communication Studies and Theater   Minor: English
    Honors: Biddeford Community Service Scholarship
                President's Citation
                Presidential Scholar Tuition Scholarship, four years
    Study Abroad: London Performance Study Program, May 1997

PROFESSIONAL DOCUMENTS

Letters of recommendation, writing samples, and theater video available upon request.

JESSICA CROWNE

3 University Avenue, Any City, State 21345   101.555.0009 (cell)
jessica-crowne@mail.com

OBJECTIVE

Teaching position working with middle-school students while pursuing a Master's Degree in Teaching at the University of Texas.
- Communication Studies
- Drama and Theater
- Language Arts

SKILLS

- Strong leadership qualities with involvement in team, group, and project work
- Extensive experience with internal coordination and communication among departments and administrative levels
- Experience with speaking, teaching, and presentations
- Intraorganizational and interorganizational communication skills involved with recruitment, personnel, and marketing services

EDUCATION

Stephen F. Austin State University, Nacogdoches, Texas
Bachelor of Arts, May 1998, Majors: Communication Studies, Theater

PROFESSIONAL EMPLOYMENT

Hardin Healthcare Corporation, Dallas, Texas, May 1998 – June 2002
Organization Analysis and Process Improvement Strategist:
- Worked with various employees to document processes and ways to improve processes using database software
- Analyzed data in different departments to have a standard process for training new employees for various job responsibilities
- Supervised the work of more than 30 temporary employees
- Worked with sales representatives to provide updated information
- Managed communication between multiple divisions within the company to facilitate a smooth transition between units

COMMUNITY SERVICE

Big Sister Volunteer, Dallas Chapter, 2003 – present
Volunteer, Hospice, Dallas and Fort Worth, 2002 – present
Volunteer Drama Coach, Youth Theater, Inc., 2002 – present
Sunday School Teacher, junior-high group, Fort Worth, 2000 – 2002

References provided upon request. Writing samples available.

JAY JUNG

3 University Avenue, Any City, State 21345
jay-jung@mail.com · 102.555.0007 cell

OBJECTIVE

Secondary Instruction
Willing to pursue teacher certification through a licensing agency

TEACHING INTERESTS

- Business Law
- Accounting
- Government
- Political Science
- Computer Technology

DEGREES

San Francisco State University
J.D. College of Law, May 2000
California License, October 2000
CPA Examinations Passed: Auditing, Tax, Accounting and Reporting

B.B.A. Accounting, May 1996
Special Honors with High Distinction   G.P.A. 3.92/4.00
Named Faculty Scholar
Accounting Department Scholarship
Ponder Undergraduate Scholarship

AREAS OF EXPERTISE

Technology: Lexis-Nexis, CCH research, PeachTree Accounting
Windows 98, ME, NT 2000, and XP

Languages: Fluent in Korean

Selected Seminars: Corporate Finance, Taxation of Gratuitous Transfers,
Problems in Tax Research, Federal Taxation II (Business)

PROFESSIONAL WORK

Accountant, Hair Art, San Francisco, June 2000 – present
Prepared state and federal income tax returns for a locally owned business.
Worked closely with the proprietors in tax planning and examining financial
records and determining best approaches in maintaining comprehensive records.

Technician, Theological Seminary, Dubuque, IA, May 1996 – May 1998
Held weekly faculty technology workshops. Resolved faculty computer
hardware/software problems, including IRQ conflicts, data restoration, and
Internet connection problems. Installed components and peripherals, including
LAN cards, RAM, modems, sound cards, printers, scanners, controller cards,
video adapters, and capture cards.

References available upon request

BUFFY CORDOVA

3 University Avenue   Any City, State 21345   (101) 555-0009
buffy-cordova@mail.com

TEACHING INTERESTS

English – Junior High and High School – with a strong emphasis in writing

SKILLS AND STRENGTHS

- Excellent written and verbal communication skills
- Ability to work both independently and as a team member
- Strong critical thinking and decision-making skills

EMPLOYMENT

Communications Director, Marketing, Inc., Dallas, Texas, 1998 – present
Assistant Communications Director, Marketing, Inc., Dallas, Texas, 1995 – 1998

- Evaluate marketing communications to ensure corporate objectives are met with target audiences
- Developed and currently maintain a global corporate communications guidebook for internal use
- Build solid working relationships with internal departments and managers as well as external vendors to ensure ongoing implementation
- Work with other departments to initiate briefs for public relations and market research agencies detailing objectives and communication activities

CURRENT VOLUNTEER EXPERIENCE

Volunteer, Corporate/School Partnership, Dallas Public Schools, 2002 – present

- Spend five hours each week working with underachieving students in the South High School reading lab; work with students on grammar usage, vocabulary development, and basic composition

Volunteer, Dallas/Fort Worth Area of Big Brothers/Big Sisters, 2001 – present

- Spend weekends and after-school time with two little sisters; work on academic assignments, leisure-time activities, and group projects

DEGREE

B.A. English, May 1995, University of Texas at Dallas, Richardson, Texas

REFERENCES

Available upon request

Judd D. O'Neal

3 University Avenue, Any City, State 21345 • 101.555.0009 (cell) • judd-d-oneal@mail.com

TEACHING INTERESTS

Teach: Physics, Economics, Psychology
Sponsor: School clubs and organizations, Student Senate, International Club

Interested in pursuing teacher licensure through alternative licensure program.

ACADEMIC BACKGROUND

University of Kansas, Lawrence, KS, August 1998 – December 2002
Bachelor of Arts in Economics and Psychology; Minor in Physics
- GPA (KU Overall): 3.66   GPA (Economics): 4.00   GPA (Psychology): 3.75
Academic Honors
- Mount Oread Scholar (awarded to top incoming freshmen): Fall 1998
- Recipient of the A. J. Boynton Scholarship (half tuition) 2001 – 2002
- Golden Key National Honor Society Nominee
- Honor Roll (multiple semesters)
- Senior Scholarship Phi Delta Theta
International Study
South America (Brazil, Paraguay, Uruguay, and Argentina): Summer 2000
- Visited many economists from South American universities
Summer Language Institute Barcelona, Spain: Summer 2001
- Studied Spanish at the Universidad de San Jordi

EMPLOYMENT EXPERIENCE

Lockton Companies, Inc., Kansas City, MO, June 2002 – August 2003
Commercial Insurance Associate
- Gained extensive knowledge of the Commercial Insurance Industry
- Worked directly with customers finding carriers to fit their insurance needs
- Exposed to all departments of commercial insurance including Loss Control, Claims Cost Control, Risk Management, Mergers and Acquisitions, Benefits, and Accounting/Finance
- Participated in unit meetings planning budgets and monitoring projects
- Learned how to read and check insurance policies for accuracy

WORK EXPERIENCE

Coca-Cola Bottling Company of Mid-America, Lenexa, KS, May 1999 – August 1999
Merchandiser
- Worked with store managers and salespeople on a daily basis in the greater Kansas City area
- Examined promotional presentation of displays and worked with marketing to use new promotional materials

CAMPUS SERVICE

Member, Phi Delta Theta Fraternity (1999 – 2002)
Elected as Philanthropy Chairman, 1999 – 2000
- Raised $14,000 for ALS (Lou Gehrig's Disease)
- Coordinated annual basketball tournament and ALS Auction
Elected Pledge Education Committee, 2000 – 2001
- Educated new members in the history of Phi Delta Theta
Elected Director of Rock Chalk Revue, 2001 – 2002
- Directed the 2002 show raising over $35,000 for area United Way

References available upon request

TASSIE A. PARTEE

3 University Avenue, Any City, State 21345   101.555.0008
Music portfolio: www.tassie portfolio.colorado.edu
E-mail: tassie-a-partee@colorado.edu

CAREER OBJECTIVE
Education
Teaching Spanish, Strings, or General Music at any level, elementary to high school

Special skills
- Musical proficiencies include electric and acoustic bass, piano, and 12-string guitar
- Public speaking; conscientious, collaborative; highly detailed, motivated to help each student achieve goals; excellent management skills; advanced technology abilities

Previous employment
Sales and Marketing - 10 years; possess strong communication and customer service skills

ACADEMIC BACKGROUND
University of Colorado, Boulder
Graduate Course Work, summers 2000, 2001   Educational Psychology and Testing
B.A. August 1992   Major: Spanish and Music Performance
- GPA: 3.48/4.00   Dean's List   Blue Key National Honor Society
- Music Scholarship – 4 years
- National Council on Youth Leadership Scholarship
- Study Abroad – University of Alicante and College of San Jordi, Barcelona, Spain

CURRENT EMPLOYMENT
Regional Manager, Lauren Inc., New York, New York, May 2000 – present
- Supervise new hires and internship students in placements in Boulder, Denver, Tulsa, Oklahoma City, and Kansas City. Work with local managers in analyzing sales records to determine profit margins and examine display locations and merchandizing advertisements. Working with three regional supervisors in organizing training seminars for retailers. Provide written reports and summary statements for corporate headquarters.

VOLUNTEER SERVICE
Families and Children Volunteer Services
- Donate hundreds of volunteer hours to United Way and Crisis Center in Boulder and Denver areas, 1995 – present. Work closely with families and children in securing temporary housing and educational and social services.
- Elected Chair, Teenagers Summer Program and Program Cochair, Learning After School, a special initiative to develop after school programs for adolescents and teenagers.

MUSIC ACTIVITIES
Current Teaching and Performance Activities
- String bass, Boulder Symphony Orchestra; Judge, Colorado All-State Orchestra selections
- Instructor, private bass lessons, Boulder, Colorado; Member, Colorado Mountain Combo

Letters of recommendation available upon request.

GEORGE T. ROVAS

3 University Avenue, Any City, State 21345   (101) 555-0008
gt-rovas@mail.com

OBJECTIVE

School Business Manager
Special expertise in:
- Finance and Budget Development
- Public Relations

EDUCATION

B.S. Degree, University of North Texas, Denton, Texas, May 1983
Majors: Business Management and Finance

EMPLOYMENT SUMMARY

Automobile Dealer Operator.. 5 years
Restaurant Entrepreneur... 3 years
Sales and General Manager, Automobile Dealerships .... 13 years

MANAGEMENT EXPERIENCE

Dealer Operator, AutoPlus, Dallas, Texas, 1999 – present
Responsibilities:
- Developed marketing strategies to attract wide audience of potential buyers
- Maintained a $5 million inventory of new and used vehicles
- Trained and motivated sales and support staff of over 30 employees
- Used positive strategies for developing successful individual salespeople
- Maintained accurate financial records and worked closely with accountants and financial analysts in preparing reports
- Attended regional and national sales meetings

ENTREPRENEURIAL EXPERIENCE

Primary partner, Athens Restaurant, Denton, Texas, Fall 1999 – present
Responsibilities:
- Collaborate with partner in financial decisions and directions for restaurant
- Consult with tax accountants, food buyers, and related professionals to create a viable, profitable business
- Manage multiple accounts and coordinate long-term planning

RELATED EMPLOYMENT

General Manager, Dallas Motor Co., Dallas, Texas 1995 – 1999
General Sales Manager, Hansen Car, Co., San Antonio, Texas, 1991 – 1995
Sales Manager, Dallas Motor Co., Dallas, Texas 1989 – 1991
Sales Staff, North Texas Chevrolet, Denton, Texas, 1983 – 1989

SERVICE

Contribute to numerous community organizations with donations or in-kind services; sponsor of various organizations for youth and support educational endeavors in community

References Provided Upon Request

AL CHENG

3 University Avenue, Any City, State 21345 101.555.0008
cheng@ugeorgia.edu   www.design/chengportfolio.edu

OBJECTIVE

Teach: Computer programming; Web production and management
Manage: Technology systems; wireless labs; multimedia for school projects

DEGREES

M.A.   INSTRUCTIONAL DESIGN AND TECHNOLOGY
                University of Georgia, Athens, Georgia, 2002 – present

B.S.   COMPUTER SCIENCE
                Georgia State University, Atlanta, May 1997

SPECIAL SKILLS

Computer Programming	Project Design	Client Consultation
Project Supervision	Multimedia Production	Needs Assessment

TECHNOLOGICAL EXPERTISE

C++, HTML, CGI scripting, and JavaScript. Built Web sites for two classes: Global Networks
and Multimedia 7:101. View at: www.educ.esl.w101 and www.educ.mm/coe5.htm
Multimedia skills: photo and authoring software, video/audio digitizing, CD-ROM Mastering

CONSULTING EXPERIENCE

Training Consultant, ALMARS Promotions, Inc., Atlanta, Georgia, Fall 2002 – present
    Hired to conceptualize and build a series of Web sites for educational programs.
    Responsibilities involve regular client consultations, budget management, and
    technical assistant supervision.

Training Consultant, East Designs, Inc., Atlanta, Georgia, June 1999 – August 2001
    Designed a multilingual computer-based training program for factory line workers.
    Experience included consulting with team management, conducting research,
    interviewing and hiring translators, computer programming, and pilot testing.

PEACE CORPS EXPERIENCE

Peace Corps Volunteer, Kingston, Jamaica, 1997 – 1999
    Developed and presented workshops to rural educators. Created special instructional
    resources and established on-going reading programs to ensure continued use of library.

PROFESSIONAL AFFILIATIONS

National Society for Performance and Instruction
Association for Educational Communication and Technology

Web Portfolio and References Available Upon Request

JUSTIN PLANO   3 UNIVERSITY AVENUE, ANY CITY, STATE 21345
101.555.0009 (cell)   j-plano@mail.com

OBJECTIVES
- To work with students in dropout prevention and at-risk programs *(interested in pursuing teacher licensure through alternative licensure program)*
- To coach athletic or intramural sports
- To sponsor club or class activities in school or in the community

EMPLOYMENT
United States Army, Microwave Radio Technician and Repairer, 1998 – 2003
Stationed in Bahrain, Germany, and Guam. Honorable Discharge, May 2003
Trained novice technicians, supervised and monitored progress. Awards received during military service:
- Support Company Soldier of the Month
- Fort Ritchie Soldier of the Month
- The Army Achievement Medal
- The Good Conduct Medal

EDUCATIONAL BACKGROUND
Stetson University, Deland, Florida, May 1998, B.A. Degree, Philosophy
Pensacola Junior College, Pensacola, Florida, May 1996, A.A. Degree, Liberal Arts
   Dean's List, Tuition Scholarship - 2 years

CAMPUS LEADERSHIP AND ACTIVITIES
Stetson letter-winner and team captain, Stetson Men's Soccer, 1996 – 1998
Referee, Intramural Basketball and Ping-Pong, 1996 – 1998
Committee Member and Student Representative, Stetson Alumni Public Relations,
   1997 – 1998
Technology Assistant, Stetson Library and Technology Center, 1997 – 1998
President, Pensacola Student Body, Pensacola Junior College, 1995 – 1996

LICENSES
Pilot's License - Single Engine Land Certification
President Elect, Deland Pilot's Club, 2002 – present

REFERENCES
Letters of recommendation available upon request
Writing samples and supervisory evaluations available

CANDY WILDE-SMITH

3 University Avenue, Any City, State 21345 102.555.0007 (cell)
candy-w-smith@mail.com

OBJECTIVE

Educational administration with special emphasis in:
- Foundation Fund-raising
- Marketing
- Public Relations and Outreach

EXPERIENCE

Home State Bank, Baltimore, Maryland, 1995 – present
- Vice President, 2002 – present
- Branch Manager, 1997 – 2002
- Training Specialist, 1995 – 1997

Current responsibilities include:
- Managing the Marketing and Community Development Department
- Overseeing and directing activities of support staff members
- Originating product concepts, developing product marketing plans, assigning production goals to all offices, developing advertising direct mail and media schedule, and coordinating bankwide staff training
- Developing and maintaining sales-training and incentive programs; directing the training of all bank personnel in sales and customer service programs
- Developing marketing action plans to meet growth and income to coincide with achievement of yearly "Stakeholders" Key Performance Indicators as part of bankwide incentive programs
- Developing budget, and implementing and adhering to annual bankwide marketing budget
- Overseeing development and maintenance of bank Web site and ensuring site adheres to bankwide strategies for product development and promotion
- Creating direct mail programs to promote all bank products and services (Monthly evaluations track household growth, product cross sales, and direct mail return ratios.)
- Overseeing development and placement of all print, radio, and television advertisements; negotiating annual media contracts

EDUCATION

Bachelor of Science, 1994, Industrial Administration and Management
 Goucher College, Baltimore, Maryland
Associate of Arts, 1992, The Community College of Baltimore County

SERVICE

Baltimore Public Library Foundation, Member and Secretary of the Board; Fund-raising Committee, Chair; United Way of Baltimore, Marketing Committee; Baltimore Banking Association, President

References Provided Upon Request

20

INTERNATIONAL SETTINGS

ENGLISH AS A SECOND LANGUAGE INSTRUCTOR

Kathy Harris

3 University Avenue, Any City, State 21345   102.555.0007
kharris@mail.com

OBJECTIVE

English as a Second Language Teacher

Personal attributes include honesty, courtesy, responsibility, punctuality, and fairness.

EDUCATION

College of William and Mary, Williamsburg, Virginia
B.A. Degree - June 2003   *graduated with distinction*
Double Major: English and Philosophy

COURSE HIGHLIGHTS

Modern English Grammar
American Writers
Women in Literature

Psychology of Teaching
Philosophy East and West
Ancient Philosophy Seminar

EXPERIENCE

Teaching Related
English Tutor, Academic Support Center, College of William and Mary
September 2002 – May 2003

Temporary English Test Specialist, College Testing Program
Washington D.C., Fall 2002

Travel
Extensive travel in Canada, Mexico, and United States
Participated in 1999 Black Hills summer archaeological dig
Semester exchange program, Université de Moncton, 2001

Language
Native English speaker
Spanish, read, write, and speak (5 semesters)
Japanese (2 semesters)

COLLEGE ACTIVITIES

Student Alumni Association
College Flute Choir
Delta Delta Delta (Chair, Community Service)
Student Volunteer, Hospice Road Races
Tutor, Volunteer Services, Special Support Office

References available upon request

TED PHILLIPIDES

3 University Avenue, Any City, State 21345 (101) 555-0009
ted-phillipides@ndu.edu *or* www.phillipides.portfolio.htm

INTERESTS AND STRENGTHS
Teaching interests
- Language instruction with nonnative speakers, including business professionals, school-age children, and young adults in a language-based institute

Strengths
- Adapt to new situations and surroundings quickly; inquisitive and self-motivated
- Conversational-speaking ability in French and Greek, comprehend Spanish
- Public-speaking skills, writing abilities, and organizational strengths
- Intensive training in communication skills; interested in working with all ages
- Available to relocate immediately; U.S. citizenship

CURRENT EMPLOYMENT
Crisis Center Program Manager, South Bend, Indiana, July 2000 – present.
  Organize programs delivered to community organizations and media outlets.
  Provide intensive training sessions to paid and volunteer counselors focusing
  on crisis situations, suicide intervention, and making appropriate referrals.

ACADEMIC BACKGROUND
University of Notre Dame, Notre Dame, Indiana, B.A. Degree, *with honors*, May 2000
    Major: Communication Studies and Theater   Minor: English
Study Abroad, May 1999, The London Performing Arts Program

TEACHING EXPERIENCE
Mayor's Youth Employment Volunteer Program, South Bend, Summer 1999
    Responsibilities included planning, organizing, and implementing community service projects for urban youth who need to develop work skills and habits.
    Fostered trusting relationships with youth to help develop ways to enrich lives.
Volunteer Teaching Experience, North City High, Michigan City, Spring 1999
    Responsibilities included observing and assisting in a skills development classroom for 100 hours. Taught and assessed small reading groups.
Swimming and Sailing Lessons, 1997 – present
    Responsibilities included teaching basic techniques to toddlers through adults.

VOLUNTEER EXPERIENCE
Tutor for English as a Second Language students, University Speaking Lab, 1998
    Taught Cambodian, Russian, and Laotian students English grammar.
Free Lunch Program, South Bend and Northern Counties, Inc., 1997 – 1998
    Collaborated with various community volunteers to prepare and serve food.

CAMPUS ACTIVITIES AND LEADERSHIP
Volunteer Recruitment Host, Admissions, University of Notre Dame, 2000 – present.
    Work with potential students and their parents. Organize tours and answer questions and concerns about campus and academic life.
Dance Marathon Coordinator, University of Notre Dame Greek System, Fall 1999
    Organized fraternities and sororities to raise money for local pediatrics unit.

References available upon request.

LEXIE SPENCER

3 University Avenue	Any City, State 21345 lexie-spencer@omaha.us.edu	(101) 555-0009

SKILLS AND INTERESTS
- Teaching skills in Elementary Education K-8 with strong academic training in science and social studies
- Experience teaching in diverse settings with at-risk and special needs students
- International student teaching experience and living with a host family
- Volunteer experience in Armenia

EDUCATIONAL PREPARATION

University of Nebraska-Omaha, B.A. Degree, May 2003 *with honors*
Major: Elementary Education   Minors: Science and Social Studies
Dean's List   President's Award for Community Service

STUDENT TEACHING EXPERIENCE

Fifth/Sixth Grade, West Elementary, Omaha, Nebraska, Fall 2002
Year 7 (Sixth Grade), Kaiapoi School, Kaiapoi, New Zealand, Spring 2003
- Implemented a positive and proactive classroom management system
- Effectively used various teaching strategies including cooperative learning and a hands-on/manipulative approach to math and science
- Guided students through checkpoint reading system and Writing Workshop
- Incorporated music, drama, sports, art, and applied technology
- Initiated service-learning program and assisted in organization of class field trips and syndicate outings
- Evaluated student behavior and academic performance in preparation for student and parent conferences

PRACTICA EXPERIENCE

Fifth-Grade Service Learning, Central Elementary, Spring 2002
Multiage Grouping, remedial reading, Hills Elementary, Fall 2001
Fifth/Sixth Grade, all subject areas, Shimek Elementary, Spring 2001

SCIENCE HONORS RESEARCH

Nebraska Center for Gifted Education, Spring 2002
- Conducted research examining relationships between science scores, gender, attributions, and attitudes toward school
- Studied implications for classroom teachers

ACTIVITIES AND AWARDS

Honors Opportunity Program	Foundation for International Education
Traveling Trunks Volunteer	Classroom Volunteer, Dyer Elementary
Nebraska Education Association	Ronald McDonald House Volunteer

OTHER

International
Armenian Reading Project, International Student Volunteers, Summer 2001
- Developed programs with high school and college students
- Worked in community-based programs during breaks

New Zealand Student Teaching, Fall 2000
- Lived with a host family and participated in cultural events
- Traveled throughout New Zealand and visited several schools

Personal
U.S. citizenship

REFERENCES

Available upon request. View my standards-based portfolio at: www.erin.teach.htm

Molly Mayflower

Present Address
International School of Brussels
19 Kattenberg
1170 Brussels, Belgium
(322) 555-67-2787   email: m-mayflower@mail.com

Stateside Address
3 University Avenue
Any City, State 21345
(101) 555-0009 or
(101) 321-9854

TEACHING INTERESTS:
Elementary teaching position in international setting.
> **Five years international experience; eight years stateside teaching experience.**
> **Qualified to work in multiage classrooms and to be a team leader.**
> **Interested in assisting in all school activities and parent-sponsored projects.**

CURRENT EMPLOYMENT
Multiage Elementary Teacher, ages 7 – 10
International School of Brussels, Brussels, Belgium, 1998 – present
> Team leader for science and math. Organize block schedules and team planning time. Teach science and mathematics using hands-on activities, manipulatives, and specialized technology applications. Create learning centers with emphasis on developing higher-order thinking strategies. Team-teach social studies and language arts. Collaborate with teachers, support staff, and administrators to create a positive and supportive learning environment for students from over 35 countries speaking 20 languages.

PROFESSIONAL SERVICE
Building level representative, Brussels International Parent Consortium, 1998 – present
Chair, Technology Committee and Resource Team for Elementary Teachers
Member, Site-based Team for Building Expenditures and Expansion
Chaperone, High School Humanities Field Trip to London, Paris, and Athens

TEACHING EXPERIENCE
Elementary Teacher, in self-contained Grade 3 classroom, 1990 – 1996
Faulkton Elementary School, Faulkton, South Dakota

Elementary Teacher, Grade 4 (3 years), Grade 3 (5 years), 1988 – 1990
Loneman School Corporation, Oglala, South Dakota

EDUCATION
Master's Degree, Curriculum and Instruction – Elementary Emphasis, May 1998
University of South Dakota, Vermillion, South Dakota

Bachelor's Degree, Elementary Education Major, Science Education Minor, August 1988
Sinte Gleska College, Rosebud, South Dakota

REFERENCES
References available at Teacher Education Center, Any City, State 21345   (101) 555-0008

AMY STEWART

amy-stewart@newark.edu
3 University Ave., Any City, State 12345   101.555.0009

INTERESTS AND ATTRIBUTES	• Experienced secondary teacher with second-language acquisition • Skilled in numerous technology applications • Qualified to teach a wide range of literature and reading courses • Committed to encouraging teamwork and creating an optimum learning environment • Enjoy working and living in new settings • Flexible and adaptable; creative problem solver
EDUCATIONAL BACKGROUND	English Education, M.A., June 1999, University of Delaware - Newark English/History, B.A., May 1996, Delaware State College - Dover
PROFESSIONAL EXPERIENCE	English Teacher, East High School, Newark, DE, 1996 – present Teach general English, American Authors survey course (grades 11/12), and an advanced composition course (grade 12). Developed curriculum for composition course, designed and implemented learning centers for general English, and served on textbook selection committee for the authors course. Work closely with teachers in history and art to teach integrated units. Collaborate in planning and instruction, and in developing and implementing assessment instruments. Supervise practicum students.
TRAVEL AND LANGUAGES	Cosponsor, Newark Area High Schools Tour of France, 1998 Toured Southern Europe and North Africa, Summer 1995 AFS Student, Orleans, France, Junior Year, 1991 – 1992 French - excellent reading skills, good conversational ability Spanish - reading knowledge
HONORS	Graduated with highest honors, Delaware State College Awarded the President's Young Scholar Certificate
PROFESSIONAL AFFILIATIONS	Phi Delta Kappa Delaware Education Association Pi Lambda Theta National Council of Teachers of English
RELEVANT DATA	Citizenship: U.S.A. Credentials: Career Planning Office, Any City, State 12345

_____ **C. T. LARA** _____

3 University Avenue   Any City, State 21345   101.555.0008 (cell)
lara@brattleboro.edu

PROFESSIONAL
INTERESTS

- Working with adolescent students in an international boarding setting
- Advising and counseling students with academic or personal concerns
- Developing educational, recreational, and social programming for international students
- Familiar and skilled in various technology and multimedia applications

DEGREES

School for International Training, Brattleboro, Vermont, June 2003
M.A. Counseling and Human Development   Emphasis: Student Personnel

Norwich University, Northfield, Vermont, May 1997
B.A. Economics and English

Lake Zurich Academy, Lake Zurich, Switzerland, May 1994
Diploma with Honors   International Baccalaureate Program

EXPERIENCE

Graduate Assistant - Student Affairs, Division of Housing, School for International Training, 2001 – present. Assist in the advising and supervision of eight student staff members in two separate units of 600 students. Implement administration policies, and work with students to resolve personal and academic concerns.

Hall Coordinator, Department of Residence Services, The University of Maine, 1998 – 2000. Responsible for the overall organization, administration, and supervision of a co-ed undergraduate hall of 400 students. Selected, trained, and evaluated a staff consisting of seven resident assistants and four clerical staff. Specific duties included facility management, counseling, discipline and advising hall government.

Resident Advisor and Instructor, Cranbrook Schools, Bloomfield Hills, Michigan, August 1997 – 1998. Responsibilities included advising and counseling students with academic or personal concerns; intervening in crisis and conflict situations; and coordinating the educational, recreational, and social programming of a 370-member residence hall. Teaching duties included senior level Economics and sophomore Composition. Maintained close communication with faculty concerning student progress.

Tutor, Hartford Public Schools Summer Reading Program, Hartford, Connecticut, 1995 – 1997. Worked with individual students to maintain their current reading level or to develop new strategies in learning to read. Interacted with diverse students in an inner-city setting.

RELEVANT
INFORMATION

International Schooling: Attended international schools, 1984 – 1994.
Lived as an expatriate in Jordan, Saudi Arabia, and Switzerland.
Citizenship: U.S. citizenship
References: Provided upon request

CARRIE HOOVER
3 University Avenue, Any City, State 21345   (101) 555-0009   c-hoover@florida.edu

INTERESTS AND SKILLS

Objective: **Director of Instruction**
Skills: **Excellent communication and organizational skills**
                Leadership experience and staff evaluation
                Strong background in curriculum development
                Experience in stateside and international settings

TEACHING OVERVIEW

Stateside: 8 years   Overseas: 4 years
New Trier High School-Wilmette   International School of Stavanger
Broward County Schools-Ft. Lauderdale   Jakarta International School

ACADEMIC BACKGROUND

Florida International University, Miami, Florida
Ph.D. Global Studies, May 2003

University of London, London, England
Fulbright Fellowship in Communication Studies, 2001 – 2002

University of Central Florida, Orlando, Florida
Bachelor of Arts in History and English, 1995

Licensure: Florida Administrative License, 7 – 12; Permanent Teaching Certificate
            Teaching Certificate in History and English, State of Illinois

LEADERSHIP EXPERIENCE

Department Chair, International School of Stavanger, 1999 – 2000
    Responsible for designing master schedule, developing budget, and working closely with
    individual faculty members.

Faculty Representative to European Council of International Schools
Curriculum Roundtable, London, England, 2000
    One of twenty-five representatives who evaluated and made recommendations regarding
    curriculum in international settings.

President, Florida State Council for the Social Studies, 1999
    Presided over a 700-member state organization interested in improving social studies
    education.

MEMBERSHIPS

National Council for the Social Studies   Society for History Education
National Council for Teachers of English   Overseas Education Association

Carrie Hoover
Page 2

TEACHING EXPERIENCE:
International School of Stavanger, Stavanger, Norway, 1997 – 2000
- History teacher, International Baccalaureate Program

Nova High School, Broward County Schools, Ft. Lauderdale, Florida, 1994 – 1997
- Honors English, American History, Geography

Jakarta International School, Jakarta, Indonesia, 1992 – 1994
- American History I and II, Advanced Placement American History

New Trier Township High School District #203, Wilmette, Illinois, 1988 – 1992
- Composition, English 10, British Literature I

GRADUATE ASSISTANTSHIPS
Teaching Assistant, Social Studies Methods, Florida International, 2002 – present.
  Instruct two sections of social studies methods classes for education majors. Evaluate
  papers and exams and prepare lectures. Guest speaker in various classrooms about
  international education.

International Student Liaison, Student Division, Florida International, 2002 – present.
  Assist foreign students with questions or concerns about course requirements, scheduling,
  living arrangements, and campus policies. Help new students cope with culture shock and
  living adjustments in a foreign culture.

SCHOOL SERVICE
Chair, Extended-Learning Program Committee, Stavanger, Norway
Member, Headmaster Interview Committee, Stavanger, Norway
Cochair, School Improvement Plan Committee, Ft. Lauderdale
Member, Curriculum Enrichment Committee-Humanities, Ft. Lauderdale
Inservice Presenter, Humanities in the High Schools, Broward County Schools
Member, Teacher Selection Committee, New Trier High School
Member, English Writing Team (state grant), New Trier High School

CURRENT VOLUNTEER AND RELATED EXPERIENCE
Guest Speaker, international travel and education topics, Miami, Florida
Volunteer Teacher's Aid, Haitian Refugee Center, Miami, Florida
Adult Tutor, Haitian Community Education Center, North Miami, Florida

Professional portfolio can be viewed at: www.carriehoover.florida.education
References available upon request

NATE HAGEDORN

3 University Avenue, Any City, State 12345   (101) 555-0009   n-hagedorn@mail.com

OBJECTIVE
Administrator — International Schools
- 16 years of combined administrative K - 12 experience
- strong background in curriculum development, technology, and finance
- executive management and organizational skills

DEGREES
Ph.D.   Educational Administration, May 1996, University of Idaho, Moscow, Idaho
M.A.   Secondary Curriculum/Administration, June 1988, University of Utah, Salt Lake City
B.S.   Mathematics and Biology, December 1985, McKendree College, Lebanon, Illinois
        International Study, Oxford, England

ADMINISTRATIVE EXPERIENCE
Assistant Superintendent, 1996 – present, Independent Schools #21, Lewiston, Idaho
- K - 12 enrollment of 22,876; instructional staff of 392; and nonteaching staff of 229. Some 62 percent of graduating seniors attend postsecondary institutions. Developed teaching partnership with International School in Rabat with teacher exchanges every two years and student exchange semesters every three years. Current initiatives include technology integration for individual classrooms with intensive staff training sessions, professional staff development, and site-based management.

Previous positions:
- High School Principal and Curriculum Director, 1994 – 1996, District #29, Rich, Utah
- Assistant Principal, 1991 – 1993, West Chicago High School, West Chicago, Illinois

TEACHING EXPERIENCE
- The American School of Barcelona, Barcelona, Spain, secondary mathematics, 1988 – 1991
- Aledo Community School District 217, Aledo, Illinois, mathematics and debate, 1985 – 1987

LANGUAGES, TRAVEL, AND STUDY
Extensive travel in Spain, France, Italy, Greece, North Africa.
Good comprehension and speaking ability in Spanish, reading knowledge of French.
Studied at Oxford in 1997 and University of London as an undergraduate.

CURRENT CIVIC ACTIVITIES
Board member, Clay United Way, 1999 – present   Founding member, Conservation Project, 1997
President, Meadows Youth Service, 1998 – present   Chair, Youth Homes, Inc., West Chicago, 1996

OTHER RELEVANT INFORMATION
Memberships: Idaho ASA, AASA, and AAIE
U.S. citizen

Complete résumé including conference presentations and publications available for review upon request. Dossier available from Career Planning and Placement, Any City, State 12345

QUINN FORD
3 University Avenue, Any City, State 12345
(101) 555-0009   q-ford@nwu.edu

OBJECTIVE
Volunteer service position focusing on education or agriculture
- Academic background in Greek, Latin, English, and Philosophy
- Training as a teaching assistant at the university level
- Good command of French; reading comprehension in German and Italian
- Willingness to live in underdeveloped areas
- Experience as a veterinarian assistant and familiarity with farming techniques

EDUCATION
Ph.D.   Comparative Literary Studies, September 2000 – present
            Northwestern University, Evanston, Illinois

M.A.   Expository Writing, June 1998, Duke University, Durham, North Carolina

M.A.   Classics, December 1994, Drake University, Des Moines, Iowa

B.A.   Classics, May 1990, Lake Forest College, Lake Forest, Illinois

TEACHING EXPERIENCE
- Department of English, Northwestern University, 2001 – present
  Graduate instructor for undergraduate composition course (2 semesters); teaching assistant for undergraduate course in Renaissance Literature (2 semesters) and survey course in World Literature.

- Harold Washington College, City Colleges of Chicago, August 1998 – May 2000
  Writing laboratory instructor responsible for individual and small-group instruction. Worked with students at various levels of proficiency.

- Department of Classics, Drake University, Des Moines, Iowa, 1994 – 1996
  Visiting instructor for introductory classes in Latin; taught one upper-level course in Greek mythology and taught a January Interim course (3 weeks) in Greek comedy.

- Department of Classics, Drake University, 1993 – 1994
  Teaching assistant for Latin I and II (2 semesters each)

ADDITIONAL ACTIVITIES
Student representative, Academic Review Committee, Northwestern University, 2002 – present
Assistant Editor, *Classics Review*, departmental publication, Drake University, 1993 – 1994
Veterinarian assistant, Animal Care Hospital, Perry, Iowa, summers and breaks, 1990 – 1998
Farm hand, crops and livestock, Perry, Iowa, 1984 – 1998

AWARDS
Paulinus Scholarship, Northwestern University, 2002 – present
Andrew Bellingham Ward Fellowship for thesis research, Duke University, 1997

References Available Upon Request

LUTHER NASH
3 University Avenue, Any City, State 21345
101.555.0009   luther-nash@uwyo.edu

PROFESSIONAL OBJECTIVE
To work in a service organization focused on building communities and action groups in Sub-Sahara Africa

OVERVIEW
    Peace Corps .... 2 years
    University Residence Halls................................. 2 years
    Federal Agency... 5 years
    State Agency... 3 years

LANGUAGES
French, Spanish, Wolof (African dialect); course work in Russian and Arabic

PEACE CORPS
Senegal, West Africa   *Environmental Education Volunteer, 2000 – 2002*
Trained over 60 teachers and school administrators from 3 provinces on environmental education strategies.
Led classroom exercises, organized pedagogy seminars, and produced workbooks for students and curriculum
materials for teachers. Coordinated a districtwide exchange across the country. Built latrines, live fences, and
other infrastructure at schools. Planted 2,000 trees.

DEGREES
University of Wyoming, Laramie, Wyoming
        M.A.   Global Studies, anticipated May 2004
        B.A.   Majors: Spanish and Finance, June 1993
        Certificate in International Business
Universidad de Sevilla, Spain, Spring 1992

UNIVERSITY OF WYOMING
Laramie, Wyoming   *Residence Hall Manager, 2002 – present*
 • Develop personal relations with floor residents as individuals and group members
 • Maintain a community that is conducive to self-discipline and study
 • Fulfill administrative responsibilities and complete schedules for floor duties
 • Advise floor government and attend hall association events
 • Attend and participate in all staff meetings and RA training sessions
 • Implement and present educational and social programs for residents

ENVIRONMENTAL PROTECTION AGENCY
Washington, D.C.   *U.S. Department of Agriculture, Assistant Project Director, 1995 – 2000*
Organized U.S. EPA training seminars for more than 1,000 recycling coordinators nationwide as part of a U.S.
EPA market development grant. Authored comparability studies on recycled products. Researched federal solid
and hazardous waste regulations under U.S. EPA contract. Authored reports for federal agency spokespersons
and for policy makers.

WYOMING DEPARTMENT OF NATURAL RESOURCES
Laramie Regional Office   *Environmental Specialist, 1993 – 1995*
Administered $650,000 in grants for compost research, production, education, and market development.
Supported the Waste Management Assistance Division in strategic planning, technical assistance, public
presentations, and program development.

References Available Upon Request

21

A FINAL
WORD ABOUT
RÉSUMÉS

Skimming through even a few of the hundred and one résumés presented in this book should make it a bit easier for you to confront the task of writing your own. Of course, a résumé is vitally important if you are looking for employment, but even if you have no urgent or immediate need for it, the time you spend creating a résumé is time well spent.

Whether you are constructing your first résumé or just updating one that has served you well in the past, take full advantage of the opportunity to record and describe your accumulated experiences and achievements. Your résumé is a professional record of real consequence. It is not just a factual statement of dates and places but an account of genuine significance that can chart progress toward goals, point to authentic abilities, suggest skills to update or strengthen, and even propose new avenues to explore. For this reason alone, any teacher can benefit from preparing a résumé and cultivating the habit of periodic updating and revision.

Although it is not a magic key, a good résumé can open doors that would otherwise remain closed to you. As a means of introduction, it can help you through the employment process, support your efforts to secure funding or grants for special projects, or highlight your particular strengths and skills for leadership roles or positions.

When the time comes to submit your résumé, you can revise, rearrange, and rework the information to make it directly relevant to your specific purpose. Revising and adapting are important processes, but they are only a means to an end. You could fiddle forever attempting to find the precise word, the ideal format, the most efficient, striking, pointed, or focused arrangement of categories, not to mention the most attractive layout, the most legible font, and the most appealing paper to convey your message. But eventually your résumé must stand alone. Except for absolute accuracy about dates and locations, and impeccable spelling and grammar, don't try to be perfect—and don't worry about final versions. As your career develops, your résumé will undergo many changes, many variations. Your goal is not to write the definitive résumé, just a positive, accurate, honest document that establishes and fosters your professional image.

BEGINNING SPANISH FOR TEACHERS OF HISPANIC STUDENTS

Pamela J. Sharpe, Ph.D.

Here at last is a valuable self-instruction program for primary and secondary school teachers who speak English only, but need some practical knowledge of Spanish so that they can work with Hispanic students. The boxed set consists of—

- A 280-page illustrated combination textbook and workbook
- 376 dialogue flashcards bound into a separate book of perforated card stock paper
- Four 90-minute cassettes
- A 92-page audioscript book

The program presents 24 lessons that start with greeting children in Spanish and introducing yourself, giving children basic instructions including taking out and putting away school supplies, participating in learning activities, praising children's good work, correcting their mistakes and behavior, questioning and comforting a child who is injured, participating in holiday celebrations and special events, communicating with Hispanic parents, and much more.

The main book's text and illustration are coordinated to match the dramatized conversations on cassette. It features many quizzes and exercises that will help you learn and retain the Spanish you need to know. The accompanying dialogue cards contain simple line drawings that depict a teacher and students engaged in a variety of classroom activities. Each card coincides with key words and phrases in the lessons and together will help you increase your memory retention.

Pamela J. Sharpe, Ph.D., is Associate Professor of English as a Second Language and Bilingual Education at Northern Arizona University in Yuma.

A quick, practical way to learn Spanish for use in a classroom setting.

ISBN 0-8120-8118-8

$45.00 Canada $65.25

Barron's Educational Series, Inc.
250 Wireless Blvd., Hauppauge, NY 11788
Order toll-free: 1-800-645-3476 • Order by fax: 1-631-434-3217
Canadian orders: 1-800-645-3476 • Fax in Canada: 1-800-887-1594

Visit us at www.barronseduc.com

Books and packages may be purchased at your local bookstore or by mail directly from Barron's. Enclose check or money order for total amount, plus sales tax where applicable and 18% for postage and handling (minimum $5.95). New York, New Jersey, Michigan, and Clifornia residents add sales tax. Prices subject to change without notice.

#74 10/05

NOTES

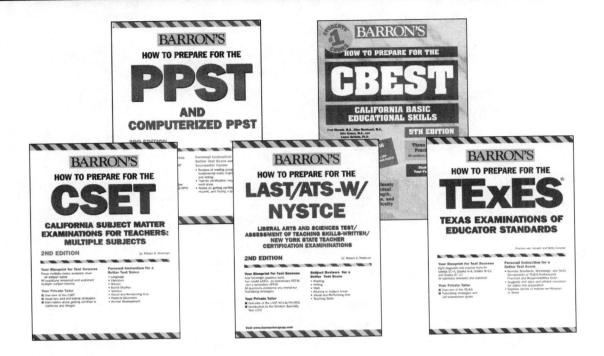

NOTES